NUFFIELD ECONOMICS & BUSINESS

Resources and Expansion

What are the limits to growth?

LONGMAN

R 26340

Copyright acknowledgements

The Nuffield Economics and Business Project team and the Publishers are grateful to the following for permission to reproduce copyright material:

The European for extracts from the articles 'Water chiefs fight tidal wave of red tape' (slightly adapted in the *European* 1.4.94, 'Cut the coat according to the cloth' in the *European* 18.8.93; Guardian Newspapers Ltd for an extract from an article by Robert Repetto in the *Guardian* 25.9.92; Times Newspapers Ltd for adapted extracts from the articles 'Bankruptcy devastates proud mining towns' by Michael Binyon in *The Times* 27.1.93, 'Fishermen block ports over quotas' by Gillian Bowditch in *The Times* 1.6.93, 'Quarries for road-building threaten wildlife havens' by Nick Nuttall in *The Times* 3.8.93, the author John Humble for an extract from his article 'Ten tips for turning the corner' in the *Sunday Times* 17.10.93, 'Tough for malts' pSC/25 in the *Sunday Times* 21.11.93, 'Gladiators' in the *Sunday Times* 12.12.93, 'Follow the green brick road' by Irene Farnsworth in *The Times* 9.3.94, © Times Newspapers Ltd 1993, 1994.

Thanks are also due to the following for permission to reproduce figures:

The British Petroleum Company plc for Figures 1.4, 1.5; British Telecommunications plc for Figure 5.3; BMW for Figure 3.9; Cambridge Econometrics for Figures 4.8, 4.9; Cambridge University Press for Figure 4.5; Earthscan for Figures 3.10, 5.1, 5.2; Environmental Business Journal for Figure 4.13; Environmental and Resource Economics for Figure 4.11; European Automobile Manufacturers Association for Figures 3.2, 3.3; Ford Motor Manufacturers for Figure 3.6; Greenpeace for Figure 4.1; IMF for Figure 3.5; Merlin Press for Figure 2.2; NatWest Review of Small Business Trends for Figure 2.3; OECD for Figure 4.10; The Official Journal for Figure 3.11; Opel for Figure 4.12; Oxford University Press for Figure 5.4; Penguin Books Ltd and Igor Ansoff for Figure 3.1; Population Reference Bureau for Figure 1.6; Rover Group for Figure 3.9; Smith New Court Securities Limited for Figure 3.4; United Nations for Figure 1.10; Vauxhall for Figure 4.13; John Wiley for Figure 3.7; World Bank for Figures 1.6, 1.7, 1.12, 4.6, 4.7, 5.5, 5.6, 5.7, 5.8, 5.9, 5.10.

Acknowledgement is also due to the following for permission to reproduce illustrations on the pages indicated:

Barnabys Picture Library for pp. 18, 39 and 103; BMW for p. 54; Bridgeman Art Library for p. 39 (top); Earthscan for pp. 24, 43, 77, 84, 89, 100; The European for p. 41; Peter Larsen and Barnabys Picture Library for p. 39 (lower); North News and Pictures for p. 51; Rover Group for p. 54; Triumph Motorcycles for pp. 58 and 106.

Cover photograph: Paul Brierley

Longman Group Limited
Longman House, Burnt Mill,
Harlow, Essex, CM20 2JE, England
and Associated Companies throughout the world.

© The Nuffield Foundation 1995

ISBN 0582 24581 8

First published 1995

Designed and typeset by
Ken Vail Graphic Design, Cambridge

Printed in Singapore by Longman
Singapore Publishers Pte Ltd

The Publisher's policy is to use paper manufactured from sustainable forests.

Contents

About this book

Resources and Expansion: What are the limits to growth? is composed of five Enquiries which explore the issue from the point of view of individuals, companies and the government. The approach of companies in seeking strategies for survival is aligned with national and global strategies to achieve sustainable development. The different perspectives are drawn together to provide an overview of the problems which arise and some possible solutions.

The effect of different political structures is discussed in the light of their responses to dealing with the problems associated with growth. The role of the market is of major significance as it both creates limits and can be used to overcome them.

A wide range of material is used to exemplify the issues and to provide a back drop for the application of economic and business principles. To assist in the process of enquiry, relevant concepts and ideas are highlighted by notes in the margin of the book.

Economic and business concepts are put to work in these Enquiries. Strategies from all areas of business management are drawn on, in order to look at both the limits and methods of dealing with them. Ideas of opportunity cost, supply and demand and elasticity are the starting points. From here you will be expected to use aggregate demand and supply, and production possibility frontiers combined with the idea of trade-offs.

Enquiry guide

The questions

Each Enquiry is intended to take about two weeks of the course and will be guided by the questions which introduce each section. The diagrammatic form of these questions shows how they relate to each other and therefore gives structure to the enquiry. They are not, however, exhaustive and there will be further questions to ask, depending on how your enquiry develops. One strategy is to look at each question in turn and ask whether there are any subsidiary ones which relate to it. Having done this you will want to put them into a coherent form and the following guide lines will assist:

■ How are these questions related to each other?
■ Which questions are most important?
■ Can they be answered with the information available?
■ What other information will be needed to draw conclusions?

The opening evidence

The opening evidence should be used together with the questions to set your agenda. It presents points of view which demonstrate a range of perspectives on the problem in hand and provides a starting point for investigation. You may agree with some of it or you may disagree but to come to a reasoned conclusion, the different angles should be explored. It is not exhaustive and will be followed up in the text. There will also be other sources which you may wish to use for reference.

The text

The text forms the main body of the book and underpins the enquiry. In general, it does not answer all the questions but it does provide a good deal of information which can be used to come to conclusions. By applying your knowledge of economics and business to the evidence, you will be using the techniques of the economist and the business specialist.

You will find 'Open Questions' in the margin. These are questions which do not have a simple answer but which should be considered carefully. They relate to issues on which no real agreement can be expected because an individual's views will depend upon their personal values. By discussing them you will be able to identify the breadth of the argument.

It is important to remember that you are being given a source of information rather than an analysis of the problems and solutions. Your Enquiry will enable you to explore and develop your understanding and form your own ideas.

Other sources

You will need to consult a range of other sources in order to carry out your investigation. Books, periodicals, newspapers and databases will all prove useful. If you have access to IT databases and CD-ROM you will find these helpful. Updating information will be an essential part of your Enquiry.

The outcome

The outcome of an Enquiry will be an analysis of the issues you have explored and an evaluation of the problems which face business, governments and the world as a whole. You will be able to look at existing strategies for dealing with the problems and evaluate their outcomes. Perhaps you will even be able to make some suggestions about improving things in future. Ideally you should find that these Enquiries have laid the foundations for evaluating future trends as they hit the headlines.

The options and the course

This book is one of a series which has been developed by the Nuffield Economics and Business Project to support Nuffield A levels in Economics and Business. These courses are examined by London Examinations. Although written for a particular course, the book may be useful to anyone studying A level Economics or Business Studies, or who is interested in the subject matter.

The Nuffield courses in Economics and Business have six options which follow that part of the course which is common to all. This book covers Option 3. If it is combined with any of the other five options it will lead to a joint A level in Economics and Business.

Acknowledgements

This book was written by Rob Dransfield, Brian Yeomans and Jenny Wales.

We are grateful to Frances Cairncross, Kerry Turner and John Dymott for their very considerable help in reading and commenting on early versions of the book.

The help and support of our administrator, Linda Westgarth, whose contributions were so many and so great that they cannot be briefly described, were essential to both the development work and the final preparation of the book for publication.

NANCY WALL
Editor

Enquiry 1: Identifying the limits

Scope

The objective of this Enquiry is to identify the limits to growth in companies, economies and the world in general. By looking at the processes involved in running a company, the first group of limitations can be recognised. Growth in all sectors is closely inter-related so the effect that companies have on the economy and vice versa need to be explored. Growth itself is responsible for creating limitations which influence the actions of everyone who makes economic and business decisions.

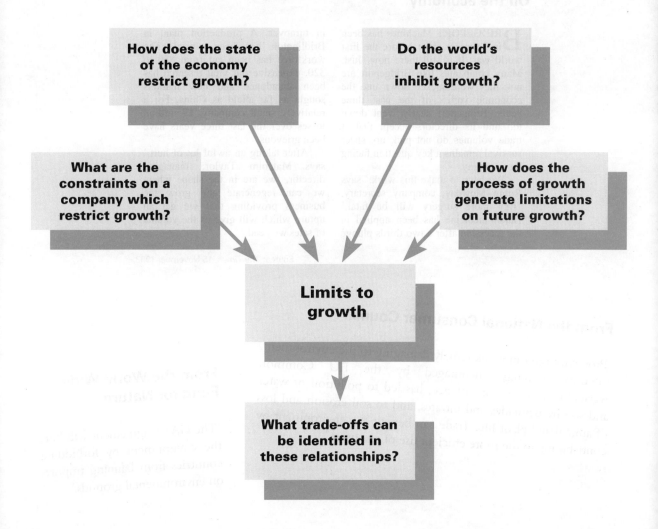

Opening evidence

On a large company

THE firm's enormous success bred arrogance, insularity and conservatism. By the mid 1980s, IBM had become so ossified, bureaucratic and inflexible that it was simply unable to rise to the competitive challenge.

Source: *Sunday Times*, 28 March 1993

From a small company

CURRENTLY we have a £12,000 working overdraft limit. We really require twice this level to function properly and make further steady growth. This request is constantly refused by the bank even though there is more than sufficient collateral to secure it. Furthermore our overdraft is reviewed on a monthly basis while this business is planning and quoting for work 12 and 18 months hence.

Source: Letter to *The Times*, 23 August 1993

On the economy

BRIDGEPORT Machines has been in Leicester since before the first world war. It is still there now. Just. Many companies like Bridgeport are not; they were sucked down into the economic vortex of the past three years. Bridgeport nearly went down too and its directors accept that if trade volumes do not pick up, sheer survival remains a key question facing the company.

'We have to make this work,' says Robin Mowday, company secretary. 'Any more surgery will be fatal.' Harsh medicine has been applied in the recession after a two thirds plunge in turnover. A production plant in Bridlington has been closed. The workforce has been cut from 850 to 320, expensive but vital research has been abandoned and new markets sought as far afield as China. For a relatively small company, £7 million losses over the last three years have been grievous.

'After taking an awful lot of hurt,' says Malcolm Taylor, managing director, 'we are in the shape where we can regenerate and grow the business providing that we get an upturn which will give us the volume of sales we need.'

Source: *The Times*, 15 November 1993

From the National Consumer Council

'Protectionism can be extremely damaging to the environment. Intensive farming encouraged by the EU Common Agricultural Policy, for instance, has led to pollution of water and soil by pesticides and nitrates, and to soil erosion and loss of animal and plant life. Trade can benefit the environment by contributing to the more efficient use of resources.'

From the World Wide Fund for Nature

'The GATT agreement will hurt the environment by forbidding countries from banning imports on environmental grounds.'

On non-renewable resources

BP's exploration team has made the company's largest find for 20 years. It is twice the size of the Forties field in the North Sea and contains more than two million barrels of oil, worth approximately £26 billion.

The field, which is located 150 kilometres east of Bogotá in Columbia, is known in the trade as an elephant because it will supply more than 250 million barrels. This one appears to be more like a whole herd.

The killing sea

THE underlying problem is the ruthless development of 'industrialised' fishing. Ever bigger trawlers with ever bigger nets have depleted the seas of cod, haddock, whiting, plaice, mackerel and herring. The destruction is intensified because sand eels and other small species on which they feed are also being caught in their billions to be turned into fish meal for intensively reared pigs and poultry.

Source: *Guardian*, 26 June 1992

Asthma – a growing epidemic

SCIENTISTS are now convinced that gas emitted from car exhausts exacerbates the asthma epidemic, which has now hit one in every seven children in Britain. This neglected epidemic puts 100,000 people a year in hospital.

It is now the greatest single cause of hospital admissions after heart disease and stroke, killing more than 2,000 people a year. It is the only treatable chronic disease to be advancing in Western countries.

Britain has the worst record for monitoring nitrogen dioxide pollution in Europe. It has only seven official monitoring stations throughout the country. The EU directive controlling the pollution lays down that the stations should be sited 'where nitrogen dioxide concentrations are likely to be among the highest … particularly "canyon" streets, carrying heavy traffic and major intersections'.

Source: *Independent*, 10 October 1993

The ozone layer – a view

THE CFC scare theory is that, when released, they rise into the upper atmosphere and shed chlorine compounds, which then break down the ozone and allow more ultraviolet radiation to reach the ground, causing an increase in skin cancer as well as contributing to global warming – the infamous 'greenhouse effect'.

So the first and most obvious question is: has there been an increase in ultraviolet radiation since CFCs came into production? No, leastwise no long term increase in UV radiation has ever been recorded. Measurements in the US taken between 1974 and 1985 show UV radiation *decreasing,* something the scaremongers forget to mention.

Ozone levels undergo violent natural fluctuations from night to day, from season to season which dwarf the worst predictions of ozone depletion by CFCs.

The stronger the sun shines, the more ozone is produced and solar activity can be measured by the number of sunspots you can count. If you plot ozone levels against sunspots, you see an almost exact match. In other words, the long term rise and fall of ozone is caused by natural fluctuations in the sun and has nothing to do with CFCs.

Source: *Spectator*, 10 March 1994

1 The tiers of constraint

What are the constraints?

Tough for malts

MACDONALD Martin Distilleries, the Edinburgh based whisky company which produces the Glenmorangie and Glen Moray malts will this week post first-half figures which analysts expect to be on target for a 'same again' performance for a full year.

In the 12 months to March, the company recorded a 50% slump in pre-tax profits to £4.35 million, blaming the recession and competitive pricing. The managing director has already warned of 'another tough year' predicting that interim results to September were likely to be below last year's £2.69m. Production of Glenmorangie is running at a third of capacity compared to the industry average of 40%.

Source: *Sunday Times*, 21 November 1993

Water chiefs fight tidal wave of red tape

TODAY, there are some 30 European Union directives or decisions controlling water. Their implementation over the past two decades has involved substantial sums of money.

But key EU officials on one side and top executives representing the industry on the other, often have conflicting views on the problems faced by the sector.

Recently, some industrialists appealed to companies to do all they could to ensure that those who make the decisions in Europe are fully aware of the cost consequences of new directives and take into consideration the consumers' willingness to pay.

The deputy director general on environment at the European Commission argued that the costs of providing water to very high standards has to be set against the advantages of the health protection that it affords. 'There are two possible points of departure for such a debate. First, can we afford to pay for the standards which are set? And secondly, can we afford not to have such standards?', he says.

Source: *The European*, 1 April 1994

Euro Disney: the future

EURO Disney executives are this weekend clustered in crisis talks with Walt Disney, the group's parent, over the future of the beleaguered French leisure park. Among the options on the table are an injection of new funds, a rights issue or even closure. Nothing according to Disney has been ruled out.

Source: *Sunday Times*, 15 August 1993

Structural benefits

When a large hospital in the Midlands awakened to the fact that in a particular outpatient department the average performance meant that the delivery of 1.5 hours of direct patient care took 7.5 weeks of administrative time a decision was taken to seek an improved strategy.

It was discovered that each patient visited the hospital six times on average – so the hospital rapidly restructured its working arrangements to ensure that the whole process can take place in one visit. Patients are happier and costs are lower. The files are retrieved once, equipment is used more efficiently and ambulance costs are reduced.

Business organisations and economies are faced with limits to growth which reflect the environment within which they function. The process of growth in both firms and economies is irrevocably linked. If firms cannot grow, economies cannot grow either, so it is important to achieve an understanding of the constraints upon them. The case studies above demonstrate how these limits affect organisations in both the public and private sectors. The four tiers, identified below, are closely inter-related:

Company constraints

■ **Company constraints:** those which stem from within the company and are associated with the running of the organisation in the market for its particular products.

Economic constraints

■ **Economic constraints:** those which result from the state of the national or international economy.

Resource constraints

■ **Resource constraints:** those which limit growth because many of the resources which we rely on are non renewable, and therefore cannot be replaced once used up.

External growth constraints

■ **External growth constraints:** those which are outcomes of growth but will limit future growth if not contained.

If company constraints are restricting the growth of firms, problems in the economy will develop. If the economy is suffering difficulties, the constraints on companies will be more severe. If firms and economies fail to take adequate note of resource constraints, the limits they face will grow increasingly hard to overcome because resources which are critical to continuing growth will have been consumed. The external growth constraints are the factors which result from growth. Populations have increased as standards of living have improved. Pollution and other environmental problems are created as industrialisation takes place. These will all create limits themselves or result in limits being placed on industry and individuals in order that further growth can be sustained.

2 Company constraints

Company constraints

Economic constraints

~~Resource constraints~~

External growth constraints

UK industry lagging badly behind rivals

British industry is lagging badly behind its international rivals with a productivity gap of about a quarter compared with France, Japan and Germany, according to a report on competitiveness produced by the Department of Trade and Industry in July 1993.

The report showed that expenditure on research and development had slipped behind in the past decade, with British industry now spending less as a proportion of GDP than Japan, Germany, France and the United States. The report described the UK's long-term performance as disappointing.

Although manufacturing productivity rose sharply in the 1980s the gap with other advanced economies had been only partially closed. The report cited the UK's 'low skills base' and the lower standards of overall educational attainment than its competitors'.

In terms of value added per hour worked, in manufacturing, the gap between Britain and three other nations – Japan, Germany, and France – stood at 20–25% while it was nearer 70% compared with the United States.

The Confederation of British Industry's national manufacturing council called in Autumn 1992 for a 5% increase in productivity each year for the next decade. However, the government is more cautious about endorsing any specific timescale for improvement, saying that the onus should be on individual industries and companies to compare their productivity month by month with the benchmark standards set by the world's best performers.

The state of affairs described above identifies some of the limitations which prevent some parts of UK industry reaching the levels of competitiveness that are achieved elsewhere. The following sections identify some of the factors which can cause limitations if they are not working effectively.

Organisational structure

Today a lot of emphasis is given to creating the architecture for business success. Professor John Kay of the London Business School defines the 'architecture' as 'the network of relational contracts within, or, around the firm'. He sees building successful relationships as a key to much business success. He cites Marks and Spencer as an example of a company with a strong architecture that depends very little on any individual or group of individuals. All too often however businesses are limited because an effective organisational architecture is not put in place.

Members of an organisation should feel proud to belong to it. Frequently they do not and this is a severe limitation to growth.

Motivation

Delayering
Decentralisation

Maintaining morale implies both motivating people effectively, and creating an organisational structure which is tailored to the needs of the business concerned. The quest for efficiency often leads to businesses changing the nature of their management structure. This can improve morale but it can also be destructive of individuals' security and sense of well-being.

Production

Lean production
Competitive advantage

Modern production is dependent on the combination of research and development, production engineering, investment funds, investment in people, and the effective use of information technology.

Technology

Effective decision making requires a knowledge of the possible avenues for increasing productivity and reducing costs. When businesses succeed in raising productivity, they are increasing output using fewer real resources. They are breaking down resource constraints and creating opportunities for growth. Just-in-time stock control, CAD/CAM, quality control and teamwork are just some of the strategies with potential in this respect.

Marketing

Marketing mix
Product life cycle

Market saturation is a problem that can face a firm all too quickly. The market may be saturated because limited demand has been quickly satisfied. Alternatively, weak marketing may mean that potential demand has not been effectively identified.

Figure 1.1 Extending the product life cycle

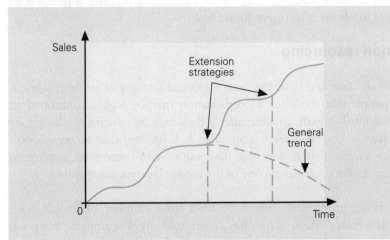

Effective marketing involves identifying consumers' requirements and meeting them in order to make a profit. Ineffective marketing involves failing to identify and meet consumer requirements at a profit. Weak marketing is thus a potentially serious barrier to a firm's expansion.

The ability to extend a product life cycle is often essential if firms are to continue to grow. Figure 1.1 demonstrates the process.

Meeting market needs

A classic example in the United Kingdom of the failure to monitor customer needs comes from the motor-cycle industry. Twenty-five years ago British roads seldom saw a foreign motorbike. Great names such as BSA, Triumph, Ariel and Norton graced the roads with heavy, slow revving, large-capacity machines. Imports from Italy in the form of lightweight, high-revving machines were rarely given a second glance by British manufacturers – they did not make them so customers could not have them. Someone had noticed these machines, however, and thousands of miles away research and development programmes were under way – Japan was about to enter the marketplace. Today the transformation is complete; motorbikes on British roads are nearly all Japanese and there are very few British manufacturers left. If the British had researched their market and found out what their customers really wanted, the position might be very different today. A revival might be on the way …

Finance

Finance is one of the biggest stumbling blocks to business expansion. It is not just a case of having enough finance, it must also be of the right type. In particular there must be sufficient cash flow to meet day-to-day trading needs.

Cash flow

The Association of British Factors and Discounters calculated that in 1993 £50 billions was owed in unpaid bills with the average business having to wait 81 days for payment.

Businesses also need to be careful not to borrow so much that they cannot meet their repayments. Rising interest rates in the late 1980s and early 1990s forced many businesses into liquidation. Any organisation needs to structure its financing carefully so as to meet its key objectives – whether they be to maintain a liquid position, or to provide funds for investment projects.

Ratios

Human resourcing

People are often said to be the most important resource of any organisation. The people that work for an organisation may be highly committed to organisational growth, or alternatively they may be resistant to change, or even have a 'couldn't care less attitude'. It is unlikely that an organisation will be successful if it does not have valued and committed employees. Human resources can create one of the biggest barriers to expansion.

A working group often needs to be a small number of people with complementary skills who are committed to a common purpose, performance goals, and an approach for which they hold themselves mutually accountable. However all too often organisations are not characterised by such solidarity. Very often groups of individuals are not clear about their aims or about the discipline needed for a common working approach. Nor will they have established mutual accountability. They may perceive themselves as being in competition with each other, which will hinder collaboration. The people involved also need high quality education and training if they are to be effective.

Entrepreneurship and management

The UK has always had a reputation for producing brilliant ideas but is generally regarded as failing to find the means to turn them into reality. Doing so usually implies that the good ideas are put into effect using innovative production strategies. But that is not on its own enough. Someone – or some people – must have the vision to see that the product will be a success, be willing to take the risks involved, and able to raise the necessary finance. Finally the management team must have the organisational skills to make the whole process profitable.

All these vital factors hang together. Overcoming company constraints usually means being able to achieve excellence on all fronts. There can be constraints anywhere in the complex systems inherent in modern business operation. The successful business will be one which has overcome a whole range of constraints in a variety of ways.

3 Economic constraints

Company constraints

Economic constraints

Resource constraints

External growth constraints

Pressures from both the national and international economies will influence growth in significant ways. In order to grow, a range of factors must be present which encourage firms to expand and develop and therefore shift out the production possibility frontier for the whole economy, as Figure 1.2 shows.

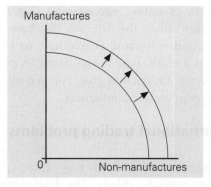

Figure 1.2 Shifting the production possibility frontier

A feeling of stability is important because uncertainty makes people unwilling to take risks, upon which the successful entrepreneurial function depends.

All adverse economic conditions, whether they be unemployment, inflation, recession or difficult trading relationships, will have a negative effect on company expansion. The following examples demonstrate how changes in the economy and government policy can affect the decision making process of firms. The effect is not simply one way. The decisions which firms make affect the state of the economy and the policy which governments have to carry out in order to influence the trends.

Unemployment

Aggregate demand

Although unemployment should reduce the cost of labour, the economic climate in which it occurs is generally not conducive to growth. High unemployment reduces the amount of consumption and therefore reduces demand because people's incomes are lower. If the market for a firm's goods seems sluggish, it is most unlikely to plan new investment and expansion.

Weak home consumption can lead to increased export effort but frequently, the trends of the business cycle are reflected in other countries and they may be facing similar conditions.

In recession, which is when general unemployment tends to occur, firms find that their sales have been hit and organisations may have to slim down in order to survive. This trend will, of course, exacerbate the situation because it will add to total unemployment and reduce consumption further.

Inflation

Pricing

Inflation is a great source of uncertainty. If a firm is to take decisions, it needs to know the price it will be paying for factors of production and what it is likely to receive for its goods in the future. This is particularly difficult for companies which are buying and selling on international markets because it will affect the value of the pound.

Costs

The treatment for inflation can also affect a firm's planning. The solution of raising interest rates increases the cost of borrowing and therefore affects the forecasts that have been made. It will also reduce consumption because people have to pay more for existing borrowing and, as a result, have less to spend. A company is, therefore, affected in two ways. Production costs rise and sales fall. Expansion is an unlikely strategy in such circumstances.

International trading problems

Changes on this front may cause problems for some and open opportunities for others. The development of protectionist policies will

Terms of trade

be appreciated by companies which face stiff foreign competition but will be a threat to a company which relies on its export trade. The freeing of trade will, of course, have the reverse effect.

The growth of production in Pacific Rim countries has caused fear among producers of similar goods in developed western markets. Costs of production are so much lower in some Asian countries that European companies have to look for another strategy if they are to continue to sell their products in the UK market. The fall of commodity prices on the other hand is welcomed by firms which use them.

Exchange rates

Movements in exchange rates can be disarming for companies which rely on trade. The effects will vary depending on the direction of the change. If the pound falls in value, imported raw materials may become more expensive but exported goods will become cheaper. If the pound rises in value, the reverse will occur.

Core and periphery

The idea of a core and periphery relates to the location of economic activity. The core is a focus for industry and commerce where much activity is concentrated. If a company is located away from this area, it is more difficult for it to grow and develop unless it is dealing with a specific market. Transport costs and person to person communication are among the difficulties which companies face. As a result, the peripheral regions of the UK find growth more of a challenge. This creates an economic problem which is extremely hard to overcome.

On a larger scale, the UK is on the periphery of Europe, which means that the country sometimes has to fight harder to retain industrial competitiveness.

Trade-offs

Manchester versus Liverpool

On 15 July 1992 Manchester airport submitted its application for a second runway which it hopes will be completed by 1998. Apart from opposition from local residents and the MP it also led to a reaction from Liverpool airport.

In February 1993 Liverpool set out plans to expand Speke airport arguing that it is already the North-West's second runway. One of the main arguments put forward was that a second runway for the area could be developed without using much extra land.

In 1992 Manchester had 25 times as many passengers as Liverpool – i.e. 11.6 million passengers – 60% of them on charter flights. It expects the number to rise to 30 million by 2005. It already has a second terminal and a fast city centre link, both sparkling new.

At the time Liverpool had three international destinations, compared with Manchester's 60. In 1992 it lost three-quarters of a million pounds with less than half a million passengers. Manchester made a profit of £47 million.

Manchester's senior managers are furious at what they see as Liverpool's attempt to constrain their growth. Sir Gilbert Thompson, the chief executive is on record as saying 'We have no objection to Liverpool increasing their business but they have no right to attempt to cap our growth.'

The Liverpool scheme would increase capacity to 9 million passengers a year. With Merseyside being classified as a poor area by the European Union, most of the infrastructure could be paid for by EU grants. It is estimated that 1,000 direct jobs are created for every 1 million passengers per year.

Sir Gilbert argued that 'They shouldn't try to stop us growing. They will get more traffic if we get our second runway than if we don't. There will be better crumbs from the master's table, they will even get loaves. They just don't understand that airlines cannot split their operations between the two airports because it doubles your costs.'

A Britannia Airways spokesperson backed up the case by saying that 'We don't want artificial constraints on growth. Liverpool's catchment area is simply not as good because half of it is in the sea. People prefer Manchester.'

Manchester's plan is something of a compromise to cope with environmental objections. The new runway will be very close to the existing one, limiting the increase in capacity: it will be in the range 42 to possibly 70 movements per hour. However, local protest groups are rallying around Liverpool's application. A local protester put forward the argument that 'Manchester's proposal will eat up 2,000 acres of land. That's crazy when there is another suitable airport nearby.'

Governments have to make decisions that affect the growth prospects of some organisations more favourably than others. Siting an airport is a problem which inevitably affects those who live nearby, the airlines and the organisations which run the airports. Environmental considerations have also to be taken into account.

Opportunity cost

In making the decision, the government has to look at the opportunity cost for the country as a whole. The costs and benefits have to be calculated and allocated. The best allocation that is achievable is where the marginal costs to society are the same as the marginal benefits to society. Figure 1.3 shows this diagramatically.

Figure 1.3 Marginal social cost equals marginal social benefit

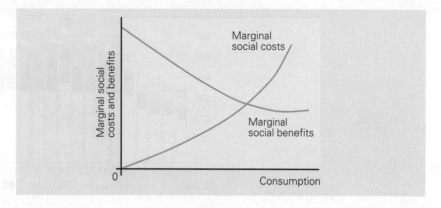

Open Question

Should growth be the main determinant in arriving at planning decisions?

The decision that is made may be beneficial for the country as a whole but may affect individual companies adversely. The expansion of Manchester airport would be at the expense of Liverpool because the former would become more attractive to industry. Small companies which depend on Liverpool airport would therefore not welcome such a decision.

4 Resource constraints

Company constraints

Economic constraints

Resource constraints

External growth constraints

Non-renewable resources are ones which are fixed in total supply and when used cannot be replaced. Their use will therefore diminish total supply. Fossil fuels and mineral deposits fall into this category.

Judging the quantity of these resources is not always straightforward because the reserves that are proved may only be a fraction of the total which is available. Figures 1.4 and 1.5 on p. 14 show the proved reserves of oil and natural gas. They demonstrate a steady increase for gas and a stepped increase for oil. The pattern is related to the process of exploration.

Resources fall into several categories. There are reserves:

■ which could be economically extracted now;
■ which are marginally economic;
■ which are currently uneconomic.

In the uncertain world beyond this there are two types of resources:

■ hypothetical – in geological formations similar to those where there are known reserves;
■ speculative – in deposits which are unrecognised.

Figure 1.4 Proved reserves of oil, 1965–1990

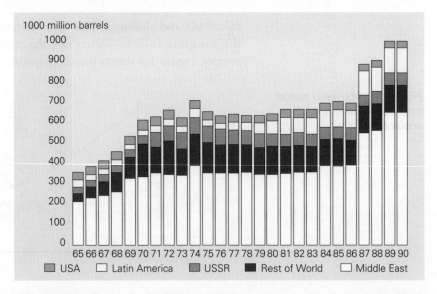

Source: BP, 1991

Figure 1.5 Proved reserves of natural gas, 1965–1990

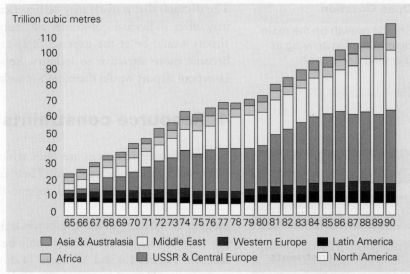

Source: BP, 1991

The degree of scarcity will, in combination with the demand for the resource, determine the price. This factor means that as a resource becomes increasingly scarce, the price will rise and therefore demand will be reduced. This, of course, works in reverse as the short case study on the use of titanium suggests.

A change of use for titanium

Raleigh, the bicycle manufacturer, has started using the scarce metal titanium to produce bikes. Titanium is an extremely light, rigid, corrosion-resistant metal. However, until recently it has been just too expensive because of the competing demand for it for defence purposes. With recent reductions in military expenditure, demand for titanium has fallen so that it has become cost effective at the top end of the bicycle market.

Provided that the market responds in this way, the use of non-renewable resources should be self limiting. Apart from the tendency for the price to rise and demand to be reduced, firms will also invest in research to use supplies more efficiently or to find alternatives.

The problems really begin to occur when there is open access. Resources that are regarded as being 'free' and therefore have no specific owner will be used to the point of depletion. This applies particularly to marine resources but there are many other examples. It will have a serious impact on future growth prospects.

5 External growth constraints

The population problem

Company constraints

Economic constraints

Resource constraints

External growth constraints

Growth has created a problem in the developing world. As the standard of living has improved, life expectancy has risen and infant mortality has fallen so total population has risen.

Figure 1.6 shows the changing pattern of population distribution which has resulted.

1993	Population (000s)	2025	Population (000s)
1 China	1,178,526	1 China	1,546,301
2 India	897,443	2 India	1,379,556
3 United States	258,328	3 United States	334,716
4 Indonesia	187,638	4 Indonesia	278,170
5 Brazil	151,989	5 Pakistan	275,170
6 Russia	149,001	6 Nigeria	246,030
7 Japan	124,767	7 Bangladesh	211,224
8 Pakistan	122,398	8 Brazil	205,250
9 Bangladesh	113,882	9 Iran	161,913
10 Nigeria	95,060	10 Russia	152,280
11 Mexico	89,998	11 Ethiopia	140,800
12 Germany	81,064	12 Mexico	137,483
13 Vietnam	71,788	13 Japan	125,806
14 Philippines	64,648	14 Vietnam	107,225
15 Iran	62,847	15 Egypt	104,607
16 Turkey	60,705	16 Zaire	104,530
17 Egypt	58,292	17 Philippines	100,845
18 United Kingdom	58,030	18 Turkey	98,744
19 Italy	57,837	19 Thailand	76,403
20 France	57,678	20 Germany	73,201

Source: *1993 World Population Data Sheet,* Population Reference Bureau

Figure 1.6 Population: the world top twenty 1993 and 2025

In 1993 several European countries were part of the top 20 but by the year 2005, these will almost all have been superseded by more rapidly growing developing countries. Current estimates suggest that world population will increase from just over 5 billion in the early 1990s to over 8 billion by 2025, and stabilise at something like that figure.

The growth of population, however, is uneven. For example, the European Union has a declining population. Only in Ireland is the birthrate at the replacement level of 2.1 per woman. West Germany in the late 1980s had the lowest percentage of population under 15 of any state in the United Nations. Italy and Spain had a reproductive rate per woman of 1.3.

In 1950 one-third of the earth's 2.5 billion people lived in the industrial world. Today with a total of 5.5 billion it is below a quarter. By 2025, when world population will be around 8.5 billion, it will be less than one-fifth. However, by this time increasingly large tracts of the globe will have been through periods of rapid industrialisation giving them the potential for mass consumption and high exploitation of resources.

Figure 1.7 Fertility rates 1970–2000

Country	Number of children per woman			
	1970	1991	2000	Year when net reproduction rate will reach 1
Tanzania	6.4	6.3	6.6	2035
Burkina Faso	6.4	6.5	6.3	2045
Zambia	6.7	6.5	6.1	2045
Bangladesh	7.0	4.4	3.3	2015
India	5.8	3.9	3.0	2015
Philippines	6.4	3.6	2.7	2010
Morocco	7.0	4.3	3.4	2015
Thailand	5.5	2.3	2.1	1995
Chile	4.0	2.7	2.1	2000
Venezuela	5.3	3.7	2.7	2005
Mexico	6.5	3.2	2.4	2010
Portugal	2.8	1.4	1.6	2030
Spain	2.8	1.3	1.5	2030
UK	2.4	1.8	1.8	2030
US	2.5	2.1	1.9	1995
Sweden	1.9	2.1	1.9	1995

Source: World Bank, *World Development Report,* 1993

As 95% of the population growth is in the developing countries, the result is that the world is splitting into two parts: an old rich world and a young poor one. The rich world accounts for an ever smaller proportion of the world population.

Figure 1.7 shows the number of children which a woman is likely to have. In the developing world rates have been much higher than in the developed world. A noticeable change has, however, taken place. If current trends persist, by the middle of the twenty-first century, the vast majority of countries will only be replacing their populations as the fertility rates are falling in most countries of the world.

The data in Figures 1.6 and 1.7 follow the observed pattern for the relationship between birth rates and death rates for a developing society.

*Figure 1.8 Development:
birth and death rates*

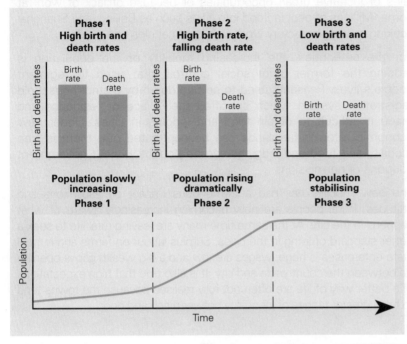

At the beginning of the evolution, Phase 1 in Figure 1.8, high birth rates are matched by high death rates, and a stable population is maintained. In the second phase, as development takes off, death rates are reduced thanks to improvements in health care, nutrition and sanitation, but birth rates remain high. As countries become increasingly developed, birth rates decline as the economy expands and as education, particularly of women, improves. This provides a rather more optimistic long term picture but in the shorter term, many problems exist and will continue to develop as population growth and economic growth run side by side.

Migration

Chinese on the move

Every year the size of China's seasonal wave of 'floating population' has been growing larger. In the weeks after the Chinese New Year at the end of January, the traditional time for contracts to be renewed, up to 90 million people stream from rural provinces such as Sichuan, Anhui, Henan, Jiangxi and Hubei to the booming coastal cities, as shown in Figure 1.9.

Figure 1.9 Migration to cities in China

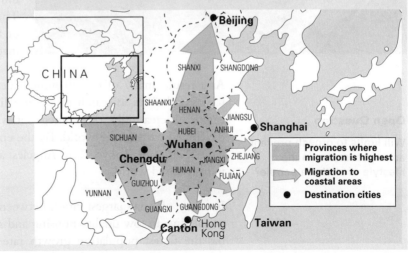

Up to a half of these may set off with no firm destination after hearing tales of lucrative urban opportunities or because of lack of work at home. Millions of people flood into cities such as Beijing, and Shanghai seeking building or factory work or jobs as nannies and maids.

For the authorities, the increasing mobility of the population is eroding the former strict social controls that used to regiment people's lives. Peasants used to be tied down by a strict household registration system which specified their place of residence and made it difficult to obtain food and lodging in cities. Under new economic reforms farmlands can be contracted out, there is free mobility and food and lodgings can be bought without government coupons or permissions.

The new mobility has had a tremendous impact on aspirations and attitudes. Rural people are now becoming increasingly aware of what happens in the city. At the same time many are leaving rural life to seek a better standard of living in the cities. Surplus labour on farms and in rural state enterprises is huge, wages are low and a big wealth gap is opening up between the countryside and city. It is also true that high expectations of a better way of life are often not fully realised because the towns tend to have greater ranges of inequality between rich and poor.

Substandard living conditions in Bombay, India.

The movement of population which is taking place in China is reflected throughout the developing world. It has been suggested that half the world's population – more than 3,000 million people – will live in 'mega-cities' by the year 2,000. In most parts of the developing world, the infrastructure simply cannot cope. The photograph shows the effects of the resulting overcrowding and inadequate services.

Open Question

Will limits to growth prevent an improvement in the lifestyle of all these people?

As a result, many of the 20 million people a year who are moving to towns and cities in search of a better life end up in slums and squatter camps. Increasingly these mega-cities are concentrating in the less developed parts of the world. By the end of the 1990s only three of the largest cities – Tokyo, Los Angeles and New York will be in the industrialised world.

In many of Asia's largest cities, between a quarter and three-quarters of people live in low quality housing and squatter camps. In Africa, which has the fastest population growth rate in the world, many cities will double in size by the year 2005 because of the high birthrate and mass emigration from impoverished rural areas.

Figure 1.10 The world's most populous cities

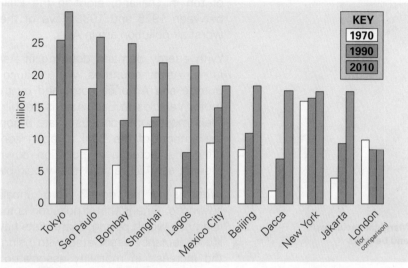

Source: UN

Increasing demand and the spread of pollution

Pay now, save later

PASSENGERS in Bangkok buses tie pieces of cloth over their faces in a vain effort to ward off traffic fumes. The middle classes in Jakarta boil their water, fearing that drinking from a tap will make them ill. Hundreds of thousands of slum dwellers in Manila drink from rivers full of human and industrial waste. Asia's booming cities are a health hazard and pollution is getting worse.

Asia is celebrated for rapid economic growth but the increase in pollution far outpaces that of GDP (see Figure 1.11).

Figure 1.11 Muck and brass

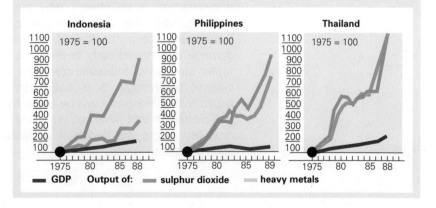

Source: World Bank

**Marginal social costs
and benefits**

According to a World Bank report, the amount of sulphur dioxide, nitrogen dioxide and total suspended particulates in the air – three of the most dangerous industrial pollutants – increased by a factor of ten in Thailand, eight in the Philippines and five in Indonesia between 1975 and 1988. Five of the cities in the world with the worst air pollution are in Asia.

With energy demand doubling in Asia every ten tears, at current rates, Asian countries will produce more sulphur dioxide than Europe and America combined by the year 2005. The number of motor vehicles in East Asia is doubling every seven years and the fuels most commonly used are among the dirtiest around. One of the authors of the Bank's report commented 'If we could merely bring the increase in pollution down to the levels of economic growth, say 10% a year, that would be a dramatic achievement.'

What is to be done? Two unpalatable arguments are often advanced. One is that if pollution is the price of economic growth, it is a price worth paying. Extremists have even argued that the rise in life expectancy associated with rising prosperity more than offsets the increase in mortality associated with rising pollution. At the other end of the scale, some greens argue that rapid growth and a clean environment are simply not compatible. If Asians want a habitable environment, they must abandon hopes of swift progress to prosperity.

The Bank's report challenges the assumption that economic growth and pollution must always go hand in hand. Some forms of industrial growth cause measurable economic losses, it says. The bank estimates that ill-health caused by pollution costs as much as $3 billion a year in lost production in Bangkok alone. 'The cost of all this pollution, in the big Asian cities is nearing 10% of urban GDP', says the report. 'The cost of clean-up is perhaps 1–2% of GDP.' Postponing the investment will raise costs later. In Japan in the early 1970s, as a result of public outcry against pollution, about 25% of industrial investment was going on pollution control; and there is now renewed pressure on Japanese industry to clean up.

If cleanliness is so cheap, why are Asian countries not already cleaning up? The bank's 1–2% calculation is based on new investment, not on the cost of re-fitting old factories and redressing damage that has already been done. But faster growth will mean faster turnover of industrial plant and new opportunities to invest in cleaner technology. It is estimated that 80% of the industrial capacity that Indonesia will be using by 2010 has yet to be installed. The decisions that Asian governments and businesses make in the next few years will decide if pollution continues to increase in a squalid upward spiral.

Source: *The Economist,* 11 December 1993

Figure 1.12 Environmental mismanagement: consequences for health and productivity

The effects of the sort of development which is happening in Thailand and other developed and developing countries are shown in Figure 1.12. Both people and industry are suffering as a result. Productivity is reduced and therefore prices will rise. The control measures which become necessary also have their costs.

Environmental problem	Effect on health	Effect on productivity
Water pollution and water scarcity	More than 2 million deaths and billions of illnesses a year are attributable to pollution; poor household hygiene and added health risks caused by water scarcity	Declining fisheries; rural household time and municipal costs of providing safe water, aquifer depletion leading to irreversible compaction; constraints on economic activity because of water shortages
Air pollution	Many acute and chronic health impacts: excessive urban particulate matter levels are responsible for 300,000–700,000 premature deaths annually and for half of childhood chronic coughing; 400 million–700 million people, mainly women and children in poor rural areas, affected by smokey indoor air	Restriction on vehicle and industrial activity during critical episodes; effect of acid rain on forests and water bodies
Solid and hazardous wastes	Diseases spread by rotting garbage and blocked drains. Risks from hazardous wastes typically local but often acute	Pollution of underground water resources
Soil degradation	Reduces nutrition for poor farmers on depleted soils; greater susceptibility to drought	Field productivity losses in range of 0.5–1.5% of GNP common on tropical soils; offsite siltation of reservoirs, river transport channels and other hydrologic investments
Deforestation	Localised flooding leading to death and disease	Loss of sustainable logging potential and of erosion prevention, watershed stability, and carbon absorption provided by forests
Loss of biodiversity	Potential loss of new drugs	Loss of ecosystem adaptability and loss of genetic resources
Atmospheric changes	Possible shift in vector-borne diseases; diseases attributable to ozone depletion (perhaps 300,000 additional cases of skin cancer a year); 1.7 million cases of cataracts	Sea-rise damage to coastal investments; regional changes in agricultural productivity; disruption of marine food chain

Source: *World Development Report*, World Bank, 1992

In some fields there is a degree of uncertainty about the exact process of pollution. There are strong suspicions and evidence which many regard as convincing that certain activities are having damaging effects on the environment.

Externalities

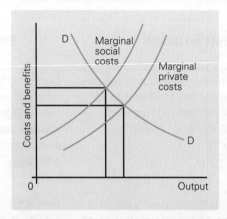

Figure 1.13 The difference between private and social costs

These are external effects from industrial activities. The company is covering the private costs and the remaining externalities are left for governments to deal with. They are the difference between private and social costs, as shown in Figure 1.13.

Three key areas of concern are acid rain, the greenhouse effect and the thinning ozone layer.

Acid rain

Acid rain is created when sulphur dioxide, nitrogen oxides and chloride are deposited in either wet or dry form. These products come mainly from the emissions of power stations and car exhausts. As they are acidic, they damage materials on which they settle. Historic buildings have been affected as well as lakes, trees, and other forms of vegetation.

Acid rain has become an international issue because it is airborne and crosses national boundaries. Damage may occur in places hundreds of kilometres away from its source.

The thinning ozone layer

Ozone in the stratosphere is important to life on earth because it protects us from ultraviolet (UV) radiation. Increasing UV radiation probably leads to an increase in skin cancer. More people have been contracting skin cancer in recent years but the fashion for being tanned may have had an impact on the figures. It appears, however, that a 1% fall in ozone leads to a 1–2% increase in skin cancer.

A more serious effect may be in the oceans. Phytoplankton, which are single celled algae, absorb a high proportion of the world's carbon dioxide and therefore assist in maintaining the balance of the atmosphere. UV radiation reduces their ability to reproduce and grow. As they are a key factor in the food chain, this could lead to a substantial reduction in fish stocks.

In Switzerland, records of changes in the ozone layer have been kept since 1926. There was little change until 1970, when a decline in its thickness started to appear. By 1988 it had thinned by 6%.

CFCs or 'chlorofluorocarbons' were introduced in the 1930s and found to have many uses because they are stable, non-flammable, non-corrosive and non-toxic. Scientists started investigating their relationship with the ozone layer in the early 1970s and found that their stability causes them to remain in the atmosphere for a very long time. By 1986 it had been confirmed that they were a source of the damage. The Montreal Protocol – which had 82 signatories by 1982 – agreed to eliminate their use over a period of years.

The greenhouse effect

The earth needs a certain amount of gases which absorb infra red radiation because they act as a blanket and help to trap the sun's rays. They keep the temperature of the earth above −19°C which would be the natural level. These gases, water vapour, carbon dioxide, CFCs, nitrous oxide and methane, have been building up in the atmosphere since the industrial revolution. Carbon dioxide, for example, has increased by 33% since 1800. The effect has been to increase the efficiency of the greenhouse and therefore retain more and more heat within the atmosphere. The effects and the relationship are still somewhat uncertain but there is a growing consensus that changes are taking place that are not merely the result of natural climatic trends.

There are considerable implications:

■ The transition phase leads to instability which results in hurricanes, tidal waves etc.
■ Marginal desert would become desert.
■ Sea levels would rise and flood areas like the Nile Delta.

Current or future production?

Figure 1.14 The trade-off between current and future consumption

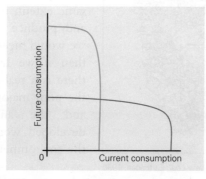

Future consumption

0   Current consumption

The desire for material development creates an enormous pressure to use current resources for current consumption, at the expense of the future in terms of both the availability of finite resources and the quality of the environment. Figure 1.14 uses production possibility curves to demonstrate the trade-off.

Trade-offs

As development takes place on a global scale world citizens increasingly demand more than the basics of food, shelter and clothing – people want transistor radios, cars, fridges, and many other resource-intensive products. Business seeks to satisfy this demand in whatever way is most profitable. In developed countries today the life of products seems to be shortening and companies make their own products obsolete by changing the design or adding new features. This is a perfectly sensible strategy if a company is interested in extending the life cycle of its product range. However, it may lead to increased consumption as people want to update their possessions. A vacuum cleaner, for example, used to last 20 years and an iron, 7 years. Today consumers replace vacuums every 7 years and irons every 3 years. All these products are using non-renewable resources, particularly oil, in their production processes.

The desire for material development becomes more urgent as wider and wider populations become more aware of the lifestyles and opportunities enjoyed by other people, as the migration of people in China demonstrated. By moving to the cities and coastal areas, people expect to find their lifestyles improving and coming closer to those in the developed world.

Changes to the environment over the past 200 years were created mainly by the industrialisation of a small part of the world – Europe, North America, and latterly Japan and other parts of the Pacific Rim (including South Korea, Taiwan, Singapore and Hong Kong). At the present time 80% of the world gross national product is produced in these industrial countries – which contain only 20% of the world's population.

If the rest of the world, without any increase in population, were to industrialise to the same extent, use resources on a similar scale, and produce similar amounts of pollution, we would meet the limits much more quickly than if we learn from past mistakes. But there is a real tension between the needs of the poor majority of the world's population, and the anxieties of many in the developed world who are concerned about the environment.

Source: Hans Moser in Mark Bryant (ed.), *Turn Over a New Leaf*, Earthscan, 1990

Enquiry 2: Use or abuse?

Scope

Abuse of the resources that contribute to growth occurs throughout the world. Whatever the political regimes, other objectives may over-ride the need for cautious management. In this Enquiry the problems are identified and the sustainable solution is sought.

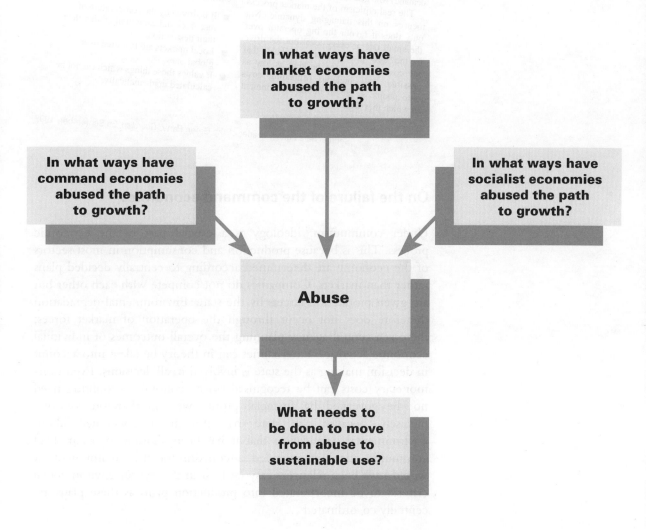

In what ways have market economies abused the path to growth?

In what ways have command economies abused the path to growth?

In what ways have socialist economies abused the path to growth?

Abuse

What needs to be done to move from abuse to sustainable use?

Opening evidence

On 'market madness'

COMPETITION is not about the 'just' price but the 'best' price in any transaction. Today, markets in any commodity are dominated by the fact that it is the buyer or seller with the most information and the most power (control of supply and demand) who gets the 'best' price.

The real criticism of the market process focuses on this damaging dynamic. Not only does it favour the big operator over the small one at every level but the drive for the 'best' price makes it inevitable that the cost of production be kept as low as possible. This includes offloading costs onto people as labour or the environment in which they live.

There may be a growing consensus that something fundamental must be done about the world's economic system – and some steps, albeit tiny, have been taken in the direction of sustainable economics, but there is still some way to go to establish a political culture which embraces the three cardinal features of a sustainable economy:

- It is driven by the conservation of resources and community rather than their destruction.
- Local markets are favoured over global ones.
- It values those things which cannot be calculated mathematically.

Source: Sara Parkin, Leader of the Green Party, *Guardian*, 25 September, 1992

On the failure of the command economies

Under communism, ideology is a crucial part of the economic process. This is because production and consumption in most sectors of the economy are determined according to centrally decided plans rather than markets. Companies do not compete with each other but are given production targets by the state. Environmental degradation therefore does not occur through the operation of market forces; there is a central agency planning the overall outcomes of individual economic activities. Externalities can in theory be taken into account in decision making as the state is involved in all decisions. Even non-monetary costs can be recognised since economic accounting need not be governed by financial profit. We can therefore say that precisely because the state has not been concerned about environmental degradation that it has been allowed to occur. Had communist ideology included a concern for the environment, it would have been relatively easy (at least in theory) for environmental criteria to be incorporated into production plans as these plans are centrally co-ordinated …

Our argument is therefore not that ideological change is not important, merely that it is not enough on its own.

Source: Michael Jacobs, *The Green Economy*, Pluto Press, 1991

A view from the past

God forbid that India should ever take to industrialisation after the manner of the West. The economic imperialism of a single tiny island kingdom [Britain] is today keeping the world in chains. If an entire nation of 300 million took to similar economic exploitation, it would strip the world bare like locusts.

Source: Mahatma Gandhi, *Young India*, 1928

Small is beautiful

What is the meaning of democracy, freedom, human dignity, standard of living, self-realisation, fulfilment? Is it a matter of goods or of people? Of course, it is a matter of people. But people can only be themselves in small comprehensive groups. Therefore we must learn to think in terms of an articulate culture that can cope with a multiplicity of small scale units. If economic thinking cannot grasp that, it is useless. If it cannot get beyond its vast abstractions, the national income, the rate of growth, capital/output ratio, input/output analysis, labour mobility, capital accumulation, if it cannot get behind all of this and make contact with human realities, of poverty, frustration, alienation, despair, breakdown, crime, escapism, stress, congestion, ugliness and spiritual death, then let us scrap economics and start afresh.

Are there not indeed enough signs of the times to indicate that a new start is needed?

Source: A.F. Schumacher, *Small is Beautiful*, Abacus, 1973

On sustainability

Economics throws light on the meaning of sustainable development because the environment and the economy necessarily interact. Economic systems impact on the environment by using resources, by emitting waste products to receiving environmental media, by changing the aesthetic functions of natural and built environments and – constituting the 'new' environmental challenge of the 21st century – by altering the global life support systems on which we all depend.

Sustainable development is feasible. It requires a shift in the balance of the way economic progress is pursued. Environmental concerns must be properly integrated into economic policy from the highest (macroeconomic) to the most detailed (micro-economic) level. The environment must be seen as a valuable, frequently essential input to human well being. Sustainable development means a change in consumption patterns towards environmentally more benign products and a change in investment patterns towards augmenting environmental capital.

Source: David Pearce, Anil Markandya, Edward B Barbier, *Blueprint for a Green Economy*, Earthscan, 1989

1 What is balanced growth?

Is this balanced growth? ...

In January 1992, Andrei Yablokov, the Russian government's adviser on the environment, made the first official attempt to chart environmental problems in the 15 republics of the former Soviet Union. He reported that the Communist Party's attitude to pollution had been near catastrophic and that the Soviet military-industrial complex had simply no regard for anything except its goal – Soviet power.

Pollution may be a significant factor in the fall in life expectancy in Russia from 70.4 years in 1964 to 69.3 in 1990. In some badly polluted cities it had diminished to just 44 years.

Some of the disasters are as yet unseen – or exist to become future shocks. Pipelines may rupture or earthquakes may occur because of excessive pumping of oil or water from deep wells. According to the report, in 20 years time, the city of Moscow will be badly threatened by underground water flooding because of a past disregard for geological structures. Pipeline ruptures account for between 7 and 20% of oil extracted, with the losses totalling millions of tons.

Radioactive lakes, created over the years by waste from the Soviet nuclear weapons programme, are at risk from earth tremors that may send the polluted waters into the Caspian Sea and cause an environmental disaster comparable to Chernobyl.

Aluminium factories in Uzbekistan have produced uncontrolled wastes that are now affecting fruit-growing areas. Lakes around the Urals city of Chelyabinsk, the centre of what was the Soviet nuclear industry, are oozing with plutonium. Heavy use of pesticides has poisoned the rivers.

Dioxins are present in mothers' milk in Moscow and the Chernobyl accident has rendered much of the produce of the Ukrainian and Belorussian countryside inedible.

... Or is this balanced growth?

'In Scandinavia, prosperity is closely associated with social justice, social security and the development of the welfare state. The term "welfare" is associated with a concept of overall well-being. We regard prosperity not only as signifying economic growth and material welfare, but including employment for all, environmental quality, gender equality, and a meaningful life. The win-win aspect of this definition is that this approach has also proved a successful strategy for economic development.

Prosperity and welfare imply more than the satisfaction of material needs. Policy goals include equal access to education, safety in the workplace, safe-guards against unreasonable job losses, and the chance to take part in the development of the company or organisation.

Universal healthcare must be included in our concept of prosperity, given that few people can meet the cost of medical treatment from their own pockets.

Traditionally, economic growth has meant producing more goods, by using more natural resources, by placing additional strain on an already fragile environment. This pattern can not be repeated uncritically on a global scale. Recent research has taught us that perpetuating such economic growth is neither necessary nor possible for prosperity. Growth does not always mean more goods, it can mean better goods.

Our economies do need growth. But it must not reduce the environment and resource-base. We need growth that leads to quality of life for all, not congestion, pollution and over-use of resources. A radical shift in our economies can only be accomplished in co-operation with labour unions and others who fear marginalisation.

Technological breakthroughs will be needed in many areas if we are to make the transition to sustainable development. One problem is that many needs that could lead to new areas of human activity do not lead to private demand in a market. However good the markets are at allocating resources efficiently and effectively, they cannot build community purpose or instil social responsibility.

We need to see knowledge as the ultimate resource and engine of growth and change. It is not natural resources in themselves which give wealth, but how we use them. If resources could make us wealthy, we could have reached today's standard of living millions of years ago.' – Gro Harlem Brundtland, the Prime Minister of Norway, at the London Business School, November 1993

Creating a balance?

Russia and Scandinavia demonstrate opposite ends of the spectrum when it comes to trading off a country's objectives with the care for the environment and the potential for future growth.

Creating balanced growth is not simply a matter of business enterprises increasing the quantity of goods and services to meet the current needs of the world's peoples. It also involves many important questions and issues such as:

■ How output and income are generated – for example do we exploit

resources to maximise current consumption or do we think about the future?
- How income and output are shared out – for example are we content simply to raise total national income or are we concerned to make sure that individuals and groups do not suffer from the growth process?
- How sustainable are existing and future resources given current production patterns?

By taking these factors into account when making decisions about future strategies for an economy, balanced growth is more likely to be achieved. The nature of government, however, seems to have little effect on the outcomes. The command economies which existed before the fall of the Berlin Wall often generated more pollution than the market economies of the West because looking after the environment was not on its agenda.

2 Pathways to growth

There are as many pathways to growth and development as there are societies. In this section therefore we set out to introduce some of the major justifications and criticisms of particular routes to growth.

The capitalist model

The late eighteenth and early nineteenth centuries saw the development in Western society of systems of thought which identified hope and progress with advances in science, technology and industry.

Adam Smith is particularly associated with developing a rationale for capitalist economic growth. Smith's theory of historical progress has four stages, based on the development of the economy: hunting, pasturage, farming and commercial society. In the *Wealth of Nations* (1776), Smith was centrally concerned with the analysis of economic advance ('the progress of opulence in different ages and nations') and with understanding its problems and its causes, including increases in the division of labour and the stock of capital accumulated. Smith showed how business and individual enterprise could contribute to the well-being of economic society.

Smith identified a propulsive force that will put society on an upward growth path and a self-correcting mechanism that will keep it there. The propulsive force was the 'desire for betterment' – or the profit motive. In Smith's words 'it impels every manufacturer to expand his business in order to increase his profits'.

The main road to profit consists in equipping working people with machinery that will increase productivity. Thus the path to growth lies in what Smith called accumulation, or in modern terms, the process of capital investment. Because of increased productivity, society's output grows.

The rising demand for working people pushes up wages. As people become better off they become healthier and mortality rates fall. More people would become available to swell the working population. As a result the demand for products would increase and the rising working population would prevent wages from rising and eating into profits. Because profits are sustained we have a self-correcting mechanism that enables growth to be maintained.

We can illustrate market-led growth in Figure 2.1 as an engine providing a propulsive force and a set of tracks that serve as a self-correcting mechanism enabling growth to take place.

Figure 2.1 A propulsive force and a self-correcting mechanism

At the same time competition between producers in the market place keeps prices down and ensures that goods are produced in line with consumer requirements. If a baker tried to charge more than competitors, trade would disappear, or if employees asked for more than the going wage, they would not be able to find work. If landlords sought to exact a higher rent than others with property of the same quality then they would get no tenants.

The limitations of capitalist growth – a Marxist critique

Since the time of Adam Smith the path of capitalist growth has not been smooth and sustained. Periods of boom followed by slump indicate that the self-correcting mechanism does not operate smoothly.

During the nineteenth century the British economy expanded at an average of about 1% a year. But progress was very bumpy. It would run up quickly for four or five years, fall back for two or three, have a

Business cycle

couple of years when nothing much happened, and then have another growth spurt. Each cycle would be slightly different in timing and depth, but it seemed inevitable that there should be cyclical fluctuations.

During the last quarter of the nineteenth century, capitalist industry was drawn into a fresh technical revolution. Like the first, the second industrial revolution changed essentially the source of power for production and transport. Alongside coal and steam, petrol and electricity henceforward played their part in driving the wheels and the machinery. This power revolution transformed the whole of industrial life. At the same time steel became more and more the basic industrial material. The chemical industry underwent its first big development.

Structural change

This industrial revolution at the end of the nineteenth century proved a powerful stimulant to the centralisation and concentration of industrial capital. A large minimum size, or large optimum size, came to be seen as an inevitable natural barrier to entry into an industry. The new techniques of production favoured concentration. Thus electrical power made possible the synchronisation of factory work and the introduction of the conveyor belt. New divisions of labour favoured the integration of concerns both horizontally and vertically.

Because of the need to assemble a substantial amount of fixed capital in order to produce under optimum conditions of profitability, industrial concentration, by putting great resources in the hands of a relatively small number of capitalists, enabled them to carve out a bigger and bigger place for themselves on the market and to drive out of it large numbers of small and medium sized manufacturers.

Because of the risks involved in putting together huge sums of capital, capitalists began to look at ways of restricting competition in order to prevent price falls and hence falls in profits. Large companies got together in a range of anti-competitive ways e.g. through 'gentlemen's agreements', price-regulating associations, cartels, trusts and holding companies.

At the same time banks were growing in size and joining together leaving a small number of very large financial institutions. Through shareholding, these financial institutions spread out their interests so that they were masters of banks, insurance companies, industrial, commercial and transport companies.

Marxist economists viewed these events as a threat to society because of the power that it put into the hands of the few. A mere 200 families, either working as individual units or in groups, controlled much of the industrial capital of the world.

Monopoly power

Figure 2.2 Net margins of profit on turnover, USA, 1956

	%
All companies	5.2
Companies with a turnover of:	
US$ 1–5 million	2.2
US$ 5–10 million	3.3
US$ 10–50 million	4.2
US$ 50–100 million	5.4
US$ 100 million and over	6.9

Source: Earnest Mandel, *Marxist Economic Theory*, Merlin Press, 1962

In order to reduce risks, monopoly capitalists restrict competition between themselves. A monopoly rate of profit is established, higher than the average rate. Monopoly super-profit results from raising the selling price of the monopoly sectors above the cost of production, and is possible because these monopolies are superior in productivity to small and medium-sized firms operating on a smaller scale. For example, figures for profitability based on scale in 1956 in the United States were used to reinforce the argument – see Figure 2.2.

Monopolies were regarded as fetters on economic progress because they:

■ deliberately restrict production. Monopolists have a vested interest in failing to supply the market to capacity in order to increase their profits.
■ suppress or delay the application of technical innovations. Large corporations tie up a lot of capital in existing machinery and equipment. They will be reluctant to see this investment being wiped out by the 'white heat' of changing technology.
■ permit the deterioration in the quality of goods. Large concerns with only ineffective competition to worry about may produce sub-standard products because they can get away with it.

On a world scale, production comes to be dominated by a smaller number of monopoly capitalists. The effective internationalisation of production, through world division of labour, carried to the extreme, is however combined with the retention of national frontiers and hence international competition. This leads to periodic explosions of imperialist wars. The competition that now exists between monopolies can be described as that of a permanent state of war interrupted by frequent truces.

Assessing the critique

Despite this tendency towards monopoly, the developed world has failed to reach the scenario described. Many companies are vast in terms of turnover, but they often face fierce competition from others in a similar position. Oligopoly is as likely to lead to rivalry in terms of prices and products as to the formation of cartels, which are, of course, against the law in most developed countries.

The growth of large companies in capital intensive industries also has a significant advantage. As fixed costs are spread over higher levels of output, the average cost will fall, so providing that the market is competitive, the price will fall. The optimum output level for the motor industry is two million cars per year. Considerable concentration is therefore required to achieve such scale.

The threat of monopoly power is one that the developed world has been aware of throughout much of the twentieth century. This has led to legislation designed to reinforce the protection from such exploitation by large organisations. It is, of course, not always successful and some restrictive practices still go unchallenged.

Monopoly legislation

Figure 2.3 The growth of small businesses

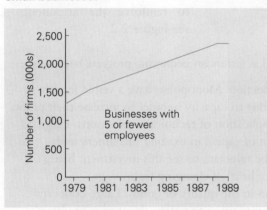

Source: National Westminster Bank, *Small Business Trends*, Volume 3 No. 1, June 1993

The small business is also becoming increasingly important. A significant feature of both of the recessions since 1979 has been the number of jobs lost in large organisations. During the 1980s the small business sector in this country experienced a 70% expansion to a stage where it represented 17% of the UK gross domestic product and 35% of private sector employment. Figure 2.3 reflects this pattern.

These developments, combined with the fact that capitalist countries have had the highest growth rates, tend to contradict important aspects of the thesis.

Alternatives to the capitalist model of growth: central planning

Golub

Slavenka Draculic, the Yugoslavian writer, tells how she finally realised that there was no future for communism, in her book *Forward to the Past*. She argues that communism foundered in a soggy mire of scratchy brown lavatory paper. She describes the coarse, dark sheets of 'Golub' she used in her childhood, then the soft, pink rolls eventually achieved by 'socialism with a human face' of the 1970s, then the day, in 1985, when she stood with her 17-year-old daughter in a chemist's shop, arguing bitterly because the recent price rises meant that they had had to go back to Golub. Her daughter refused point blank to adopt this symbol of poverty and Draculic knew then that it was all over: 'This was how the communists lost: when the first free elections came in May 1990, the entire younger generation voted against Golub, against shortages, deprivation, double standards and false promises.' – Slavenka Draculic, *Forward to the Past: How We Survived Communism and Even Laughed*, Hutchinson, 1992

The collapse of communist regimes in eastern Europe in the early 1990s had, according to historians, many complex causes. In looking for political causes, they point out that Mikhail Gorbachev, who became leader of the Soviet Communist Party in 1985, allowed criticism of the state after 50 years of repression. The process of *glasnost* (openness) made the workings of the government less secretive. This allowed new political parties to set themselves up. New nationalist groups, began to demand independence. This *glasnost* spread through eastern Europe like wildfire.

However, some people argue that perhaps the most important factor behind the fall of communism has been the failure of the economic system. Communist parties failed to achieve one of their central objectives – to improve living standards. Perhaps we should add 'to improve living standards as fast as people would have liked'. Living standards for many did rise considerably between the pre-communist days and the 1980s. However, by this time many Eastern bloc citizens were aware that they were lagging considerably behind the West.

For 60 years the Soviet Union had a highly centralised economy: most of the important decisions were taken by the central planners in Moscow. Prices were set by government rather than by the actions of consumers and producers. It was Stalin who originally introduced the policy of centralisation. During the 1920s and 1930s, Stalin rapidly expanded industrial production and brought most firms under state ownership. He also introduced a system of 'collectivised' farming. Land owned by better-off peasants was confiscated and turned into large holdings owned by the state or collectives of peasants so that eventually 99% of all land was collectively or state owned.

At first the system was successful in industrialising the Soviet Union, providing full employment and boosting food production as well as leading to other aspects of growth. In the long term, however, it stifled enterprise because all decisions were taken centrally. Bureaucrats began to build their own empires and lose touch with the needs of consumers.

The system came to be based on state capitalism and the concentration of industry. For example, the Ukraine produced much of the iron, steel and coal, while the Baltic republics specialised in producing electrical goods.

Raw materials produced in one part of the country had to be transported thousands of kilometres to be processed in another, which wasted time and energy. Agriculture suffered from shortages of machinery parts and difficulties in transporting produce. Energy resources were wasted recklessly. For example, in many towns, central heating systems were switched on and off from a central point so that individual householders had no control over the temperature in their own flats. They were left to regulate temperatures by opening and closing the windows.

Emphasis was placed on military expenditure and scarce resources were channelled into this area. Levels of productivity in industry were low compared to those in the West, so Eastern bloc countries began to run large trading deficits.

Although everyone was employed, underemployment was rife so that people were spending many unproductive hours at work. Prices rose faster than wages and living standards were relatively low. People had to queue for basic goods such as bread, butter and meat. Many goods had to be bought on the black market at inflated prices.

In the summer of 1991, the communist system in the Soviet Union was overthrown, to be replaced by a Commonwealth of Independent States. Mikhail Gorbachev was replaced by the more radical reformer Boris Yeltsin.

Socialism and co-operation

Many interesting ideas on pathways to growth have come from the developing countries where ideas are partially shaped by conditions of poverty and dependence on the world's developed countries. Co-operatives have proved a successful method of mobilising the rural poor and enabling them to become both more productive and self-sufficient in a broad context. The Bangladesh Rural Advancement Committee (BRAC) shows how a successful venture can improve the lives of a rapidly increasing number of people. It was set up in 1972 as a relief project. By 1990 it had a membership of 350,000 people in 210,000 households in 3,200 villages. Its budget was $22 million and it employed 4,200 people.

Co-operatives can be extremely successful in mobilising the population but in many cases are relatively small in terms of the economic development of the country as a whole.

The Bangladesh Rural Advancement Committee

BRAC focuses exclusively on the landless, mobilising them into co-operative groups, who then plan, initiate, manage and control collective activities that lead to self-reliance. The activities cover a wide range of areas, reflecting BRAC's belief that the complexity of the problems demands a simultaneous search for solutions in many different fields including:

Functional education – the key process which villagers are required to complete before groups can be formed. In 1990, 43,000 villagers were attending this course in 1,800 centres. The course itself consists of sixty lessons taught in two one hour classes a day, six days a week for two and a half months. It has also been used by other organisations and the government.

Non-formal primary education – for unenrolled children or drop-outs, using a specially developed curriculum focusing on basic literacy, numeracy, health and environment. By the end of 1990 126,900 children, 70% girls, were taking this course in 4,025 schools.

Training – especially in the areas of human and occupational skills development, the former comprising consciousness raising, leadership development, project planning and management and functional education teacher training, the latter imparting skills in poultry keeping, agriculture and a variety of trades.

Meetings and workshops – groups hold weekly meetings and inter-group meetings for a variety of purposes. Higher level committees of group delegates meet monthly to discuss issues that cannot be solved locally, e.g. wage bargaining, protest action, access to government services.

Health – since 1980 BRAC has reached 12 million or 85% of Bangladesh's rural households with its simple oral rehydration therapy for child diarrhoea (responsible for 33% of the country's infant mortality). This has now developed into BRAC's Child Survival Programme, consisting of a primary health care programme, continuation of the oral rehydration work and assistance to the government in its immunisation and vitamin A distribution work.

Para-legal services – since 1986, villagers chosen by their group are trained to act as para-legal counsellors in such matters as land conflicts and registration, civil rights and unfair practices.

Generation of income and employment/credit support – agriculture, irrigation, fish culture, poultry, livestock, bees and other rural industries have all been promoted as income earners against which credit has been given. So far $10 million has been lent with a repayment rate of 96%.

The organisation also runs:

- The Women's Production Centre and six shops to sell their products
- BRAC Printers
- Cold Store Enterprise
- Garments Industry

Source: Paul Ekins, *A New World Order*, Routledge, 1992

3 The end of an illusion

The process of economic growth involves pushing the production possibility curve outward. To do this means increasing the factors of production – land, labour and capital. Increases in population, the opening up of new frontiers and markets have acted as a dynamic to growth. The development of new technologies has always fuelled the growth process as well. Figure 2.4 shows the effect of growth on the aggregate supply curve.

Figure 2.4 Growth and aggregate supply

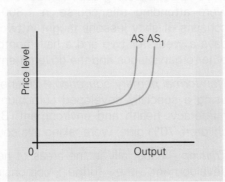

Of the three systems for running an economy, which have been discussed above, none have succeeded in achieving growth without incurring costs. The shift in the aggregate supply curve, which represents growth taking place may be counter-balanced by destruction of the environment which reduces a country's ability to grow in future.

Abuse in market economies

The following case study describes a city which the Conquistadores discovered in the Valley of Mexico on 8 November 1519.

City of 'enchantments'

During the morning we arrived at a broad causeway and continued our march towards Iztapalapa, and when we saw so many cities and villages built in the water and other great towns on dry land and that straight and level causeway going towards Mexico, we were amazed and said that it was like the enchantments they tell of in the legend of Amadis, on account of the great towers and cues of buildings rising from the water, and all built of masonry. And some of our soldiers asked whether the things that we saw were not a dream ... With such wonderful sights to gaze on we did not know what to say, or if this was real before our eyes with Montezuma, we went to the orchard and garden, which was a marvellous place both to see and work in. I was never tired of noticing the diversity of trees and the various scents given off by each, and the paths choked with roses and other flowers, and the many local fruit trees and rose bushes, and the pond of fresh water ... We must not forget the gardens with their many varieties of flowers and sweet-scented trees planted in order, and their ponds and tanks of fresh water into which a stream flowed at one end and out of which it flowed at the other, and the baths that Montezuma had there, and the variety of small birds that nested in the branches, and the medicinal and useful herbs that grew there ... I may add that on all the roads they have shelters made of reeds or straw or grass so that they can retire when they wish to do so, and purge their bowels unseen by the passers by.

We saw three causeways that led into Mexico ... We saw that fresh water which came from the Chapultepec to supply the city, and the bridges that were constructed at intervals on the causeways so that the water could flow in and out from one part of the lake to another. We saw a great number of canoes, some coming with provisions and others returning with cargo and merchandise; and we saw that one could not pass from one house to another of that great city and the other cities that were built on the water except over wooden drawbridges or by canoe ...

Mexico City in the sixteenth century.

Source: Bernal Diaz, *The Conquest of New Spain*, Penguin, 1963

Contrast the above account with a description of the same area which appeared in the *Man and the Biosphere Program* submission to the United Nations in 1984.

A city of our time

The Valley of Mexico is located in the extreme south of the central mesas and covers a surface area of 9,600 square km. The land is suitable for crops, fruits, natural pastures and man-made grasslands. The main land use problems are linked to the lack of soil nutrients, erosion, salinity, alkalinity and flooding. Over-grazing and excessive deforestation have led to extensive resource depletion in the valley.

There are also serious pollution problems, due as much to the wastes resulting from domestic daily activities as to wastes from large industrial zones. Pollutants are emitted from industry, 2 million cars and 'natural' dust storms which originate in the areas around the dried-up Lake Texcoco in the NE of the city and which blow human waste from these sewage outlets all over the Federal District.

Mexico City today.

Waste disposal is a major problem. The metropolitan area produces 6,000 tons of solid waste each day, of which only 75% is collected.

The rest is scattered throughout the city, most of it on untreated dumps. Those in 'marginal' settlements near the dumping grounds are most severely affected by these wastes and there is resulting environmental degradation, through methane production, and through soil and water contamination.

The population, currently about seventeen million, is expected to reach about thirty million by the year 2000. Today water is transported long distances across mountainous regions to the Federal District. Electrical consumption for pumping water may double between 1985–88 and then double again by 1990. At present 50% of the land surface is affected by problems of erosion. If deforestation, overgrazing and inappropriate agricultural practices continue as at present, an even more critical situation will result. The problem is compounded by continued urban incursion into highly productive agricultural land which results in a lowering of agricultural production.

Source: Sanchez de Carmona, Office of Urban Development and the Mexican Government, 'Submission to the Man and Biosphere Program of the UN', 1984

This dramatic comparison shows clearly how unregulated market activity can lead to destruction. Fortunately, controls have been introduced through much of the developed world but this does not prevent such destructive tendencies from emerging.

Despite control of river pollution, water companies are still some of the worst polluters. Welsh Water came top of these in the UK with 15 convictions for sewage leakage in 1992. One of these killed thousands of fish in the River Dee and threatened a wild-life haven.

The controls are designed to turn external costs into private costs by ensuring that companies remove pollution from their effluent before disposing of it. Figure 2.5 shows the effect of such legislation.

Figure 2.5 Turning externalities into private costs

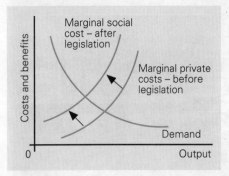

Damage is not always deliberate but may be the result of unforeseen outcomes. Unleaded petrol, which was introduced to help the environment, contains an additive to boost octane level. It is now being found in water courses and is leading to pollution. The underground tanks of petrol stations tend to corrode and start to leak. Because the additive is highly soluble, it has reached the water courses and can lead to foul smelling and tasting water. If it is to be removed, water companies will have to install new filters which will increase the price of water to the general public.

On a larger scale, pollution and environmental damage continues and, on some occasions, is given government support because of the financial trade offs between the plans that do more or less harm. Road schemes, for example, are firmly bound up with the costs involved. By building a tunnel instead of a cutting, the costs multiply several times.

A judgement has to be made as to whether that money might be better used in other ways. Inevitably opinions will differ about the relative merits of the alternatives.

Abuse in centrally planned economies

The priorities of command economies have always been different. The role of industrial production and military strength has been uppermost in the minds of the governments of Eastern bloc countries. The outcome has been that both production and military activity have taken place at the expense of people and the environment. Despite the political changes of the late 1980s, the results of these activities are still with us. The state of the River Tyecha (in the case study below) is due to the priority given to military activity. There are also many examples of the lack of concern for emissions from heavy industry.

Unless the environment is clearly on the agenda in a command economy, the problems will probably be severe. In a market economy, if resources start to run out prices will rise, so people will reduce consumption or search for alternatives. In a command economy, there is no such incentive.

Blighted river wrecks immunity 'like Aids'

THEY call themselves the walking dead. In the heart of Russia, in one of the most polluted spots on earth, a village of 6,000 people are being worn down by radiation. Their blood, liver, stomachs and brains are contaminated and their immune systems shattered by a constant barrage of rays. Even samples of teeth taken recently from a three year old child show traces of deadly plutonium.

A doctor in the village says, 'We eat plutonium, drink plutonium and breathe plutonium. More than 90% of the people living here are sick in some way. It is like a kind of Aids; it wears down your resistance to everything.'

The cause of their misery is a few dozen kilometres away along the River Tyecha which flows through the heart of the village. Near its source, amid a mass of marshes and lakes, lies one of the world's largest military complexes, a secret known only as 'Chelyabinsk 65'.

Since the plant began producing weapons grade plutonium in the late 1940s, two serious accidents and decades of dumping into the river have released 146 million curies, probably more than double the amount which spewed from the Chernobyl disaster in 1986.

After the most serious disaster, policemen were posted on the banks of the river to stop any fishing or swimming but neither they nor the locals were told why they were there.

Source: *The European*, 2 September 1993

Abuse in socialist and co-operative systems

In Africa the idea of development as self-reliance was pioneered in Tanzania in the 1960s and 70s. President Nyerere believed that the majority of developing countries are trapped in a world system that is dominated by the rich developed countries who have a vested interest in maintaining the dependent status of Third World countries in order to control world prices and commodity markets. Nyerere's alternative was to set Tanzania on a path towards self-development and socialism.

The reforms were based on a supporting structure of greater equality so that the salaries of high paid officials were cut.

Because of the importance of agriculture and the widespread poverty of rural populations, a great deal of importance was given to a programme of education and co-operative village development known as 'ujamaa', a Swahili word for family.

The objective of these changes was to reduce dependence on expensive imports, to expand local industries and to increase self-sufficiency in the countryside, so that Tanzania would become more reliant on its own resources.

The whole scheme seemed to be a perfect solution to the problems facing a developing country which did not want to industrialise in the way that the far eastern countries had already begun to do.

However, it became apparent that people did not want to be organised in this way. To establish the ujamaa villages, people had to move from the areas where they lived and many did not want to go. Human rights were seriously infringed as the unwilling were bundled into trucks and taken away. The culture of a country may well over-ride such well intentioned schemes.

The second flaw in the scheme was that all incentives were removed so instead of achieving greater output from agriculture, it actually fell. As a result the people of Tanzania are now among the poorest in the world with a low per capita income, and a high proportion living in poverty. In fact, Tanzania, fell back from being one of the countries with potential in Sub-Saharan Africa, to one of the poorest.

Dependence on internal resources can seriously limit the growth process of nations which are close to the subsistence level. Failure to generate any surplus means that capital accumulation cannot take place. India, for example, rejected the notion of self reliance because it failed to generate significant growth in the standard of living.

4 Sustainability: avoiding abuse

It appears that no one form of government can guarantee to avoid the problems associated with growth. All countries are seeking to develop further and unless new strategies are devised this will prove impossible. Sustainability has to be an objective if people are to continue to reap the benefits associated with growth.

The term sustainable development is common parlance but its definition is less straightforward and means different things to different people. The following quotations from a range of eminent environmentalists show the possible interpretations of the term.

Source: Chas in Mark Bryant (ed.), *Turn Over a New Leaf*, Earthscan 1990

What is sustainability?

'Development which meets the need of the present without compromising the ability of future generations to meet their own needs.' – Gro Brundtland, *Our Common Future*, 1987

'We can summarise the necessary conditions for sustainable development as constancy of the natural capital stock.' – David Pearce, *The Pearce Report*, 1989

'Sustainability ought to mean that a given stock of natural resources – trees, soil quality, water and so on, should not decline.' – David Pearce, *The Pearce Report*, 1989

'This does not mean that sustainable development demands the preservation of the current stock of natural resources or any particular mix of human, physical and natural assets. As development proceeds, the composition of the underlying asset base changes.' – Robert Repetto, World Resources Institute

'When we express concern about environmental matters we in effect point to a decline in their stock, on its own it is not a reason for concern ... There is nothing sacrosanct about the stock levels we have inherited from the past. Whether or not policy should be directed at expanding environmental resource bases is something we should try and deduce from considerations of population change, inter-generational well-being, technological possibilities, environmental regeneration rates and the existing resource base.' – Partha Dasgupta and Karl Göran-Mäler, *The Environment and Emerging Development Issues,* 1990

The concept of sustainable development in any of these guises raises some issues:

■ What is the role of substitution?
■ What role will the market have in dealing with the problem?
■ Is it morally wrong to leave fewer resources for future generations?
■ Can we ask for the same standards from hungry populations in the developing world?

The achievability of sustainable development is therefore going to depend upon your standpoint. If you believe that resources must not be depleted, it is more difficult to achieve than if you hold Dasgupta's view that stock levels are not sacrosanct.

The 'stock levels' that are referred to include both manufactured and natural capital. This includes the environment, natural resources, roads, machinery, housing and human capital in the form of education and training. So the ranges of interpretation of sustainability are wide. These alternative standpoints are known as strong and weak sustainability.

Weak sustainability

A constant capital stock is required to achieve weak sustainability. This means that there may be fewer natural resources but this reduction can be compensated for by an increase in education or factories. We are then passing to the next generation, the same total quantity of resources.

The environment does not count as a special component in this case. One condition which applies to all forms of sustainability, however, is that the depletion of resources that are fixed in supply must be accompanied by investment in substitutes. So if non-renewable resources such as oil and coal are used up, investment must be made in renewable sources of energy.

Strong sustainability

The substitutability of all resources which is assumed in the requirement for weak sustainability has to be questioned. The 'critical natural capital' which is essential to human survival, may not be replaceable or substitutable. Ecologists might argue that the ozone layer, global warming and bio-diversity all fall into this category because they all affect other resources which are important to human existence.

If strong sustainability is to be achieved, capital, for which there is no substitute, should be passed from one generation to the next, in its entirety.

There are two further reasons why strong sustainability should be the objective. Firstly, the precautionary approach suggests that it is wise to be cautious when there is so much uncertainty. The systems which control our environment are not fully understood and therefore, assuming that replacement of one type of capital with another will suffice, may not be an adequate approach to long run sustainability. Secondly, if natural systems are damaged, the effects may be irreversible. The reduction in bio-diversity is the obvious example but combined with uncertainty, the effects of other actions may be similarly destructive.

Resources which are finite but which can be replicated or substituted may be of less significance in the overall picture than those which cannot.

As the amount of oil is depleted, two things happen. The price will rise so it will be used more sparingly and therefore total exhaustion will be delayed. Firms which rely on it will work increasingly hard to find a substitute, either for the fuel or for the equipment which uses it. Substitutes for oil are a distinct possibility but the ozone layer and white tigers are more of a problem. Once white tigers have gone, we cannot replace them and once the ozone layer (if the pessimists are right) has thinned sufficiently, much of the world will have to change its life style. Oil is a private good, for which the price mechanism functions reasonably effectively, whereas white tigers resemble a public good which is provided by an external source and will need protection if it is to continue to exist.

The limits to growth will therefore depend upon the understanding of sustainable development. If we must pass an unadulterated set of resources to the next generation, the limits are closer than if a more flexible approach is taken.

Calculating our effect on the environment

In the calculation of national income or Net National Product, the amount of physical capital that has been used up is accounted for in the 'capital consumption allowance'.

Another way of writing this would be:

$$NNP = C + S - Detr.K_M$$

Where:

NNP = Net National Product
C = Consumption
S = Saving
$Detr.K_M$ = Deterioration of manufactured capital

If an equivalent calculation is to be carried out for the amount of natural capital that has been used up, a method of measurement has to be devised. The amount must then be deducted from NNP to produce a figure for the 'green' national income or gNNP.

The amount of natural capital which is depleted is referred to as $Dep.K_N$. The amount of natural capital which is degraded is referred to as $Deg.K_N$.

These are used in combination with the equation above to calculate green national income.

$$gNNP = C + S - Detr.K_M - Dep.K_N - Deg.K_N$$

By using this equation, a judgement can be made about the degree of sustainability which is being achieved. The way in which this is done is explained in detail in *Blueprint 3* by David Pearce, Kerry Turner and Timothy O'Riordan, Earthscan, 1994.

Enquiry 3: Strategies for survival

Scope

In this Enquiry strategies for the survival of a firm lead into an investigation of the ways in which the environment is incorporated into decisions or turned to advantage. Survival is then explored in the light of the range of different perspectives which has developed in recent decades.

> **What strategies might a firm employ to survive?**

> **Why might today's strategies and those of the past impinge upon the future?**

> **How have the perceptions of environmentalists differed in their solutions to such problems?**

> **What strategies have been devised for allowing continued growth without damaging prospects for the future?**

> **What would the pessimists advocate?**

Opening evidence

L'Escargot Anglais

The company, along with many others, started breeding snails five years ago. With a 40% mortality rate, most firms didn't last long. Mr Vaughan, the founder of L'Escargot Anglais, discovered that there was little advice on how to achieve success. He had to decide whether to cut his losses or invest time and money in research and development. Eighteen months later, he had turned the business round and become a snail breeding expert with some of London's best restaurants among his customers. His expertise has won him lucrative contracts including being snail breeding adviser to the Czech and Slovenian governments.

Gladiators

TELEVISION profits have almost doubled in two years, from £21.9m in 1991 to £42.5m in the year to October, and there is more to come. But Gerry Robinson, the Granada Group's Chief Executive, has also proved that cutting costs is perfectly compatible with raising output and quality. Last year, Granada was nominated for 12 British academy awards while making more programmes than ever before. It supplied more than a quarter of the ITV network's originally commissioned British programme hours: by far the highest of the ITV companies.

But with only 11% of ITV's £1.5 billion annual advertising revenues, themselves coming under pressure from satellite television. Robinson knows that Granada needs a sizeable slice of the lucrative southern England pie, hence his takeover bid for London Weekend Television. 'We have done extraordinarily well from a northern base, but coming from that location we have to fight twice as hard,' he says.

LWT has a slightly higher share of ITV advertising, but Robinson has no doubt that as a stand-alone company, it is more vulnerable than Granada to the winds of change in television. 'On its own LWT is too small to grasp these new opportunities,' Granada says. 'Indeed, it risks being marginalised.'

Source: *Sunday Times*, 12 December 1993

Finding the right formula for a commercial green world

MACRO social and economic change will continue, while profound concern will be voiced about the environment and reflected in ever tighter regulation, with ever more bureaucracy to add to the already heavy costs on those of us who are wealth creators. The more traditional industries will be forced to change technology because of environmental and competitive pressure. They will look to science to help them solve their development of high technology but the force of the bioscience revolution is only just beginning to be felt, while the electronic industry also has a long way to go. As we approach the year 2000, there are no easy answers, but there are signposts.

We shall all have to be more selective in the areas in which we compete. We cannot afford to try to out-do each other right across the board. We shall have to focus on those areas of particular technological and commercial strengths.

The pressures on our cash flow from competition, overcapacity and demands for environmental improvement will continue to be significant and, in Europe at least, this must lead to a process of rationalisation and consolidation.

We are going to have to get closer to our customers and become much more adept at solving their problems. At the same time, we must ensure that we get paid adequately.

Improving environmental performance is not an optional extra; it is an absolute prerequisite if we are to have a continuing licence from the general public to operate.

Source: Denys Henderson, Chairman of ICI, *The Times*, 17 March 1993

The world problematique

The Club of Rome arose in 1968 from these considerations. At present, it comprises one hundred independent individuals from fifty-three countries. It has absolutely no political ambition. Its members represent a wide diversity of cultures, ideologies, professions and disciplines, and are united in a common concern for the future of humanity. It chose as its initial theme 'The Predicament of Mankind'.

From the outset, the Club's thinking has been governed by three related conceptual patterns. The first is to adopt a global approach to the vast and complex problems of a world in which the interdependence of nations within a single planetary system is constantly growing. The second is to focus on issues, policies and options in a longer-term perspective than is possible for governments, which respond to the immediate concerns of an insufficiently informed constituency. The third is to seek a deeper understanding of the interactions within the tangle of contemporary problems – political, economic, social, cultural, psychological, technological and environmental – for which the Club of Rome adopted the term 'the world problematique'.

The world problematique has become, as it were, the trademark of the Club. We define it as the massive and untidy mix of intertwining and interrelated difficulties and problems that form the predicament in which humanity finds itself.

Source: A. King and B. Schneider, *The First Global Revolution*, Simon & Schuster, 1991

It is not natural resources in themselves which give wealth, but how we use them. – Gro Brundtland

British Steel's investment

LIFE has changed from hell to heaven for 900 employees at British Steel's coke and iron works in Port Talbot, South Wales. This is the result of British Steel's award-winning £70 million rebuild of the blast furnace. Advanced technology, involving the use of the largest crane in Europe, enabled the old blast furnace to be rebuilt in 149 days. The rebuild has achieved higher productivity and improved quality while meeting the most stringent environmental standards. The cost of pollution control measures, including water recirculation and noise reduction equipment, was in excess of £12 million.

Source: *The Times*, 9 March 1994

Sustainable development : The UK strategy

Because of the ways in which the environment is shared, collective action is necessary. There are certain specific principles to be taken into account in pursuing this:

- Decisions should be based on the best possible scientific information and analysis of risks.
- Where there is uncertainty and potential serious risks exist, precautionary action may be necessary.
- Ecological impacts must be considered, particularly where resources are non-renewable or effects may be irreversible.
- Cost implications should be brought home directly to the people responsible – the polluter pays principle.

Judgements have to be made about the weight to put on these factors in particular cases. Some environmental costs have to be accepted as the price of economic development, but on other occasions a site, or an ecosystem, or some other aspect of the environment, has to be regarded as so valuable that it should be protected from exploitation.

Source: *Sustainable Development: The UK Strategy – Summary Report*, HMSO, January 1994

1 Inter-relationships

The range of *limits* which face us all, companies, countries and individuals, were discussed in the first Enquiry. These limits range from the very specific problems which face companies to the global problems which are the concerns of international organisations. What ever their size, they affect everyone in varying respects.

The company which decides to restructure may:

■ use resources more efficiently;
■ make people redundant;
■ create a more challenging working environment;
■ make more profit for shareholders.

The government which agrees to reduce the use of CFCs may:

■ cause cuts in employment in the industry;
■ boost companies which are producing alternatives;
■ help in the reduction of skin cancer;
■ make refrigeration more expensive for the developing world.

The individual who decides to use public transport and sells the car may:

■ improve the quality of the air;
■ reduce congestion on the roads;
■ reduce oil companies' sales;
■ reduce employment in the car industry.

These demonstrate some simple inter-relationships which will occur as people and organisations change their habits in response to the changing environment. In order to cope, it is necessary to devise strategies for survival. The objective will be to improve the situation for the company, the individual or the world in general. Some may lose from these changes but others may gain, especially if they look for new opportunities.

Risk

Worm farming

The ragworm has long been the bait used by sea anglers. They have, for centuries, been dug from the seashores by anglers and professional diggers alike. However, in recent years, the practice has grown and environmentalists and local authorities have become concerned about the effects.

Seabait, a company from Lynemouth in Northumberland started to grow ragworms by aquaculture with research and development assistance from Newcastle University.

In its first seven years the company's output of worms has increased seven-fold and the company now produces 17 tonnes each year. They are sold to anglers at £2.50 for a 75 gram pack of about 15 worms.

A handful of farm-grown worms.

The company has recently received The Queen's Award for Environmental Achievement. Not only is it helping to maintain the country's seashores but its use of inputs also reflects an awareness of the environment. Waste products from Alcan Primary and Power UK have been put to good use. The tanks in which the worms grow are built on a bed of concrete that has been produced by using waste ash from Alcan's power station, and warm water, which results from the cooling process, feeds the tanks. Alcan have been very supportive of the whole venture, which is sited on what was waste land adjacent to its plant.

This initiative has benefited many, especially as it has created new jobs in one of the UK's unemployment black spots.

Private and social costs and benefits

Many companies are not as fortunate as Seabait, which has snatched an opportunity to build up a market for a product which was approaching a limit. No-one had grown the worms before. Any that were sold had been dug from the wild and this was the cause of the problem. Digging for ragworms had become a legal issue because its scale had grown and increasing damage was being done to the seashores. By filling this gap in the market, Seabait helped both themselves, the environment and the anglers.

Organisational structure

The limits faced by many companies are not environmental but organisational or technical. To overcome some of the problems which are created, companies may need shock treatment or they may require a concerted effort over a long period of time. Organisational problems may only be solved by a rapid change in the structure of the company, whereas research and development will provide solutions to product problems, for example in the pharmaceutical industry. Whatever strategy is used, the effects of the actions of a company will not stop at their boundary fence. The implications for stake holders may be considerable.

2 Corporate strategy for survival

Forming strategy

In the past, firms have often laid down a set of objectives, designed to lead to corporate success. In recent years, companies have found that this is not sufficient because the world in which they work has become more changeable. As a result planning has become more discontinuous and companies have to be prepared to make complete changes of direction when the need arises.

The development of a strategy is a necessary part of the process when confronted with problems which are outside the company's existing framework. If this does not happen the firm will drift into greater and greater difficulties.

By identifying its *strategic portfolio*, a company decides on the areas of business in which it sees its future. Figure 3.1 shows the sample growth vectors for the motor industry. It shows how the possibilities range from products of a similar type in both related and unrelated technology to those which are quite remote from existing activities. Various methods can be employed to decide which strategy is the most appropriate but in the final analysis the executive must make the decision in the light of the circumstances in which it functions.

Figure 3.1 Sample growth vectors for a car manufacturer

Product / Customer	Related technology	Unrelated technology
Same type	Motorcycles, lawnmowers, intra-urban personal vehicles	Electric home appliances
Firm its own customer	Gas turbine engines, wheels, transmissions	Paint, glass, tyres, etc.
Similar type	Farm tractors and machinery	Computers for small business
New type	Diesel locomotives, missile ground support equipment	Petrochemicals, drugs

Source: Igor Ansoff, *Corporate Strategy*, Penguin Books, 1987

This must be combined with a *competitive strategy* which defines the way in which the company plans to approach the market. It may be through market-share maximisation, growth, market differentiation or product differentiation.

The more complex the company, the more complex the strategy will be. The requirements of a firm which buys and sells will be relatively simple whereas a conglomerate will need to look closely at the synergy between members of the group if its strategy is to be effective.

Both the *strategic portfolio* and the *competitive strategy* will be affected by the type of limit that the company is facing. The range which was identified in Enquiry 1 suggests that a company's policy will be influenced in different ways depending on these specific needs.

Pushing out the limits: merger

Economies of scale

A major issue concerns company expansion. For many companies, expansion is necessary if they are to reach the minimum efficient scale. To be competitive in world markets, it is often essential to produce on a scale which is sufficiently large to spread fixed costs as thinly as possible. The motor industry is the commonly stated example as it is suggested that an output of two million cars per year is the minimum efficient scale for volume car production.

Figure 3.2 Motor industry in Europe: market share

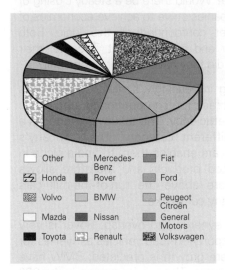

Source: European Automobile Manufacturers Association

Sometimes the easiest way to achieve larger scale production is to merge. This will bring financial and marketing economies of scale, and perhaps other advantages too. First the many small producers which set up the motor industry amalgamated; more recently in the UK, Ford took over Jaguar and BMW took over Rover. The European motor industry's market share is shown in Figure 3.2.

Within Europe, only Volkswagen is producing on a scale which approaches the optimum, as shown in Figure 3.3 on p. 54. Others, such as Ford and the Japanese companies, are producing on a world-wide scale and their European operations are just a part of the total. There remain a number of other companies, some of which are in the luxury end of the market and therefore operate successfully on a smaller scale, others of which are probably below the optimum for cost efficiency.

Ford have now gone one stage further in the internationalisation of the company, making structural changes which put the responsibility for each category of car into the hands of a specific regional group of the company. If other car makers want to use this approach, there may be further mergers in the industry.

Figure 3.3 Motor industry in Europe:
output per year

Other
Honda
Volvo
Mazda
Toyota
Mercedes-Benz
Rover
BMW
Nissan
Renault
Fiat
Ford
Peugeot Citroën
General Motors
Volkswagen

0   500,000   1,000,000   1,500,000   2,000,000

Output per year

Source: European Automobile Manufacturers
Association

 Why did BMW buy Rover?

There is over capacity in the European car industry and all producers fall below the optimum output of two million cars per year. There had been many suggestions as to the possible solution to this problem. Should two of the large companies merge? Would there be a steady closing of the less efficient factories as companies strive to achieve economies of scale? The BMW/Rover takeover confounded all this logic. Both companies sell cars to the upper end of the market. Together their output is less than 1 million. What did they have to offer as one unit?

Mass market cars are becoming increasingly similar, so price has become a much more significant factor in competition strategy. This means cutting costs and raising efficiency. The takeover produces a car company which is in a different category. The company's position as a producer of quality cars enables them to find a niche in the market for their differentiated products and therefore allows them to charge prices which are above the run-of-the-mill cars which feed the UK's large company car market.

In the takeover, there was both synergy and overlap. Rover is very strong in the growing market for sporty off-road vehicles as well as for small front-wheel drive cars, where growth is predicted. BMW have neither of these products in their range. The overlap comes in the 800 and 600 categories in which both companies have successful models. Rover has a wealth of traditional brand names which evoke memories of days when motoring was motoring – MG, Riley and Austin.

The UK industry also had much lower wage costs, which could be used to encourage more modest claims in Germany. Rover's growing share of the UK market also made the company attractive. It was the only firm in Europe to have a rising share of the contracting market (during the early 1990s recession).

The two firms together produce a new type of car company – one which aims at a specific sector of the market and has a wide range of cars. Perhaps this suggests that future restructuring may take a different view of the conventional wisdom concerning size and strategy in the industry.

Demerger

Mergers are not always the answer as ICI found when the company planned its strategy for the future. Their business fell into two distinct sectors and an unexpected decision was made to demerge in 1993.

Sometimes the split is not as straightforward as this natural divide. A company may have to seek efficiency by divesting itself of subsidiaries in order to concentrate on the core business, achieving focus by exploiting its competitive advantage.

Focus

ICI and Zeneca: the great divide

ICI is a company that has grown and developed since it was established in 1926. A dramatic announcement was made 66 years after its formation. The company would be divided into two groups: bulk chemical production, which continued to be known as ICI and the bio-science sector which took the name Zeneca.

The logic behind the division was that these two sectors required very different strategies, so by functioning as separate companies each could pursue their own priorities.

The chemical industry is, in part, an undifferentiated, bulk business. One tanker full of sulphuric acid is much the same as another so competition can only be on price. Any company involved must therefore drive costs as low as possible if it is to be competitive. Much of this had already been carried out. In the two years before the demerger, the company had taken 20% out of the cost base of the chemicals and plastics side of the company. The plan was to reduce its concentration in parts of its portfolio. The highly competitive bulk chemicals sector was to be scaled down by selling some the businesses involved and concentrating on higher value added products. The whole organisation was streamlined. The regional management superstructure was removed by closing its separate national head offices and cutting the staff in London.

The changes were required because Dow Chemicals in the US achieved sales of £211,000 per employee, whereas the equivalent in ICI was only £99,000. The company planned to become 'performance orientated, cost-conscious, with no frills'.

The bio-science sector, which has become Zeneca, produces drugs and other related products in a high margin industry where research and development are essential for success. This sector had been too dependent on one drug, which had produced 50% of sales but was rapidly losing its place in the market because its patent had expired. The new company needed investment if it was to re-establish itself as a leading drug company. The strategy which was set in place aimed to produce one new drug every year. Investment in research and development was therefore crucial to the achievement of the objective.

The company's chief executive did not rule out the possibility of a merger between Zeneca and another pharmaceutical firm. The pressure for research and the costs involved combined with the increasing pressure on health care costs throughout the world means that companies need to be large and concentrated to have any degree of success in the industry.

Figures 3.4 and 3.5 show that both companies maintain a significant position in the world market but with specific concentrated activity might move higher up the league. If Zeneca were to merge with any of the others, it would take a powerful position in the market.

Figure 3.4 Top 10 chemical companies

	Sales $bn
1 Hoechst	28.5
2 Bayer	25.6
3 BASF	24.1
4 Du Pont	22.8
5 Dow	18.8
6 ICI	15.7
7 Rhône Poulenc	14.5
8 Ciba-Geigy	14.2
9 Shell	11.2
10 Enichem	10.9

Source: Smith New Court

Figure 3.5 Top 15 pharmaceutical companies

	Sales $bn
1 Merck and Co	4.0
2 Glaxo	3.7
3 Bristol Myers-Squibb	3.3
4 Hoechst	2.7
5 SmithKline Beecham	2.4
6 Sandoz	2.3
7 Ciba-Geigy	2.3
8 Lilly	2.2
9 Johnson & Johnson	2.1
10 Pfizer	2.1
11 Roche	2.0
12 Bayer	2.0
13 Rhône Poulenc	1.9
14 American Home	1.9
15 Zeneca	1.6

Source: IMF

Re-engineering

Change management

As companies develop, they tend to carry their existing structures with them. This may be inappropriate because an organisation which is suitable for a small company will probably be unable to cope with the more complex planning and decision making of a larger company.

At this point the need for change appears. It is also true that as markets become increasingly competitive a large staff with many administrators may become a luxury that the company cannot afford. 'Downsizing' has become the euphemism that is popularly used to describe the process of reducing staffing levels. Many companies, from Unilever to BP have undergone downsizing or restructuring schemes.

The example of Ford, which faced heavy losses and reorganised the company internally from the top levels of administration to the production process, shows how it can be necessary to make such changes in order to remain competitive. It demonstrates how a company must look at every stage of the process if it is to succeed in the marketplace.

A new shape for Fords

By 1992, Ford was in deep trouble. The world car market was in recession and Ford was suffering particularly badly. Jaguar's deficit of $400m and a reorganisation and redundancy bill for the same amount exaggerated the situation, but Ford of Europe was no longer the jewel in the crown of the world-wide company, as shown in Figure 3.6.

Figure 3.6 Ford of Europe: profit and loss

Year	Profit/loss
1987	+ $989m
1988	+ $1,460m
1989	+ $1,190m
1990	+ $145m
1991	– $1,080m★
1992	– $1,300m★

★ includes Jaguar
Source: Ford

Jacques Nasser, commonly known as 'Black Jac' because of his habit of turning red into black – or losses into profits – was brought in to sort out the company. At Ford Australia, he had increased productivity and quality by 40% in two years, while cutting the workforce from 16,000 to 9,000.

Ford's problems stemmed from rigidity in management. Staff, from the foremen upwards, had great loyalty, but were resistant to change. As a result, his plans included streamlining the decision-making process by simplifying the management structure so that people had greater responsibility. By working in this way, the objective was to meet customer needs more quickly and effectively.

Costs had to be cut on a broader front than just in the management structure. Components suppliers were unhappy at the Ford announcement that costs of supplies were to be cut by 10% over a period of three years. The unions suspected that labour would fall below the level of the planned cuts which would reduce the existing Europe-wide workforce by 10,000 to 83,000.

The world-wide company underwent a complete restructuring as well. Cars were to be produced for the global market. No longer would Fords be made for Britain, they would be made for the world. To do this, responsibilities were allocated to specialist centres around the world. The Escort and Fiesta were to be made in Britain while the Granada range would be the responsibility of the large car division in Michigan.

This would save at least $3 billion a year because all the automotive processes would be integrated and duplication eradicated. It had been predicted that the lower production costs would feed through over a period of years to the showroom, resulting in a fall in price that would cause an increase in demand. Production of small cars could therefore double from the existing 1.5 million.

Open Question

Are large companies more or less likely to act in the public interest than small companies?

Technology for survival

A TRIUMPHant revival

The UK motorbike industry died a death because it could not compete with the mass produced bikes from Japan. Many would have suggested that the only strategies for revival had to be either a hand-made highly specialist product or an emulation of the Japanese motorbike industry. The methods of the past, when the machinery took eight hours to reset in order to produce a different model and parts sat on benches waiting for these changes to be made, were no longer viable.

Instead the UK now has a small growing company which sells bikes at competitive prices and has a range of ten different models despite only having sales of 8,000 bikes in 1993. How has this been achieved?

In 1988 a Midlands property developer bought the name 'Triumph' and invested £70m of his own money in a new plant. It was equipped with the latest machinery that overcame all the problems of the old British motorbike industry. The introduction of cell production speeds up the whole process and in a very short period of time the whole production line can be switched from making the tourer to the big three cylinder bikes or any of the others in the range.

By using a modular approach, components can be put together in different ways to create different models. Now the company can meet most customised requirements and respond rapidly to demand. This adds to the company's flexibility, which is important because it is working in the 'fashion' market.

Triumph's revival is unusual. Its existence results from one person who not only had sufficient funds to establish the new firm but was also prepared to forgo a quick return. Few banks would have been prepared to make such a long-term investment without more rapid results.

Product life cycle

Triumph demonstrates how a strategy that uses technology can be effective in overcoming the limits to growth within existing situations. If the market for products changes or the competition develops more effective production methods, it is essential that a company can adapt to meet the requirements. The new company has achieved this in two ways. Firstly, it has re-entered the market because technology has enabled it to produce goods that the market wants with a cost structure which allows it to compete with much larger firms. Secondly, the equipment that has been installed means that response times to market changes are shortened and new products can therefore be on sale extremely rapidly.

Using all the strategies

Some companies survey the market place, identify where the market is going and devise effective strategies to take them there. They defy recession, use technology to produce at competitive prices and marketing skills to keep them in the public eye. Benetton is a prime example.

Cut the coat according to the cloth

DESPITE the recession and tough competition the Italian leisurewear group Benetton continues to go from strength to strength.

A state-of-the-art clothing factory at Castretta in north east Italy is the latest symbol of the group's confidence in the future. The $32 million plant, designed by architects Afra and Tobia Scarpa, is supported by what looks like part of a suspension bridge.

Benetton technical director general, Renato Tardidi said: 'If it was a traditional factory it would require at least 800 blue collar workers and 200 white collar workers. Here we will employ around 200 highly skilled technicians and fewer than 100 unskilled workers.'

Since Benetton's foundation as a small family run business in 1965 the company has expanded at an astonishing rate. Despite the labour saving technology, the group has never reduced its personnel, as chairman Luciano Benetton is quick to point out: 'This plant is the most advanced in the world in terms of labour costs. It proves that in Italy, if you are capable of innovating, even the textile industry can compete with countries where labour is five times cheaper.'

The company continues to maintain a high profile through controversial advertising campaigns. The extension of their retailing activities has pleased foreign investors. The new lines, such as shoes, watches, sunglasses and other accessories have helped boost profits. The group's three year plan provides for growth in turnover from $1.6 billion in 1992 to $2.6 billion in 1996 said Guiseppe di Maria, a stockbroking analyst in Milan.

Source: *The European*, 18 August 1993

Benetton has succeeded in maintaining a growth path through recessionary times. Ford set about a process of restructuring to overcome the problems which recession and other structural factors had created. The policies that they had adopted all fall into the list of advice 'for turning the corner'. This list was originally created for companies which were trying to overcome recession but it holds good for any firm which is aiming to overcome the limits which can constrain future developments.

Ten tips for turning the corner

1 *Spend a day with the customers*
Listen – what makes the customers happy? Who makes the final decision to buy? How can you retain your customers?

2 *Transform customer guarantees*
Make them bold, clear, fair and relevant. Dramatically reduce the sense of risk in buying from you.

3 *Spend a day at the front line*
Work the night shift. Serve in your shops. Get close to the daily life of your front line staff. Learn the subtle truths that don't show up on reports and statistics.

4 *Empower the front line staff*
Give them more authority and information. Flatten the organisation structure. Build teams. Try trust instead of control.

5 *Train, train, train*
Service excellence calls for professionalism, self confidence and commitment. Training has a major contribution to make.

6 *Check out your competition*
What can you learn? Never knock competitors. If they are retaining your potential customers, they must be doing something right.

7 *Clear out the bureaucratic mess*
Bureaucracy is endemic and costly. Set tough targets for your department: 20% fewer reports 20% fewer meetings. Challenge every procedure manual and take a third out of those which survive. Focus on your core business and competencies by sub-contracting non-core activities to specialists. Harness the power of IT systems.

8 *Use speed as a productivity tool*
Track precisely the flow from receipt of order to delivery and drastically reduce the time taken.

9 *Measure, measure, measure*
Set standards for every aspect of quality and service. If you can't measure, you can't control. Check achievement. Measure customer satisfaction with the same dedication given to financial analysis.

10 *Live the corporate values*
The shared values in an organisation create a 'mind set' for the way things are to be done – every sale, every contact with a customer, every relationship with a competitor, every business decision.

Source: *The Times*, 17 October 1993

Looking after the environment

In the 1980s firms found themselves with a new challenge: the *green consumer*. Many regarded them as a threat rather than an opportunity but all were aware that they had to respond to the call for different attitudes to the world environment. There are, of course, costs involved in green production. They may arise from changing the technology, altering the inputs or creating community relationships where production will affect the local residents.

Internalising externalities

Green accounting

The initial response of business to environmental matters is concern about the legislation but social responsibility is now running a close second. The growing awareness of consumers means that issues that were ignored twenty years ago are now on the agenda in many board meetings. Many companies have an environmental policy. A growing number are carrying out environmental audits. The Premier Business Park initiative demonstrates how from small beginnings, greater environmental awareness can develop. The project improved the environment and lead to an increasingly profitable outcome for those involved.

One strategy which has proved successful is to reduce the amount of raw materials which are used in the production process. A Coke can, for example, now uses much less metal than in the past and many electrical products have grown smaller and lighter. Once the technology has been developed, the benefit of this approach is that it reduces costs rather than increasing them.

Premier Business Park goes green

A dingy, vandalised industrial estate in Walsall was failing to attract new companies or customers to resident firms. The future looked gloomy for Lobro Tools, a company which had invested over £1m in premises and equipment on the estate. Its owner had limited choices. By moving out, he lost the skilled labour force which he valued highly but if the company was to stay, something must done. He opted to stay and set about the revival of the estate.

With help from the Walsall Chamber of Commerce and Industry, Groundwork (a trust which specialises in regeneration schemes) and many of the occupants, the estate was given a face lift. Trees were planted, roads resurfaced, BT cables were put underground and new lighting installed.

By working together the companies have organised collection of waste for recycling. On their own, they were too small to make this viable. The move to improve the environment has led to greater interest in the gains that can be made in the future. Several of the companies have had financial assistance from BP for Groundwork to carry out 'green' audits which assess the environmental impact of energy use, raw materials, production methods, transport policy and pollution. Savings have been identified from cutting waste to reducing heating costs. The companies are beginning to see that going green is an advantage, not a burden. The next objective is to make the park the first industrial estate to receive BS 7750, the British Standard on environmental management.

3 International strategies for survival

Trade-offs between competitiveness and internalising all costs

The increase in world wide industrial activity that has taken place over the last hundred years has had a significant impact on the environment. The strategies which firms might employ in order to keep prices low and overcome the competition are not always environmentally friendly. A company is generally more interested in the private costs than the externalities which are caused by its production processes. As the awareness of these problems grew, people started to attempt to identify the causes and seek solutions.

The development of environmental thought

Concern about the environment has been on the international agenda since the 1970s. It has been characterised by two lines of thought which are shown in Figure 3.7. The first has been influenced by the work of Malthus, an economist who believed that the world population would increase geometrically while agricultural output would grow arithmetically. In other words, population would continue to double in the same period in which agricultural output would increase much more slowly. He foretold that because of absolute scarcity, the earth would not be able to sustain the population, which would therefore fall.

Figure 3.7 From limits to growth to global change

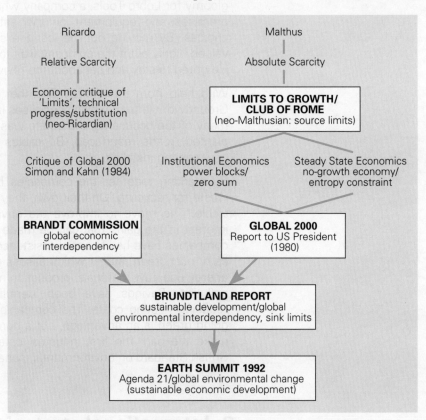

Source: Katrina Brown, W Neil Adger, R Kerry Turner, 'Global Environmental Change and Mechanisms for North–South Resource Transfers', *Journal of International Development* Vol.5, No.6, 1993

Ricardo's followers based their thought on the notion of relative scarcity which suggests that markets will have an influence over the use of resources. This implies that the problems which result may not be as dramatic as Malthus predicted. The range of views on environmental matters falls along the spectrum from technocentrism to ecocentrism, terms which have developed to describe these differing attitudes. Figure 3.8 explains the position of four points on this spectrum.

Extreme technocentrism	Accommodating technocentrism	Communalist ecocentrism	Extreme ecocentrism
A resource exploitative, growth orientated position: it is taken as given that unfettered market mechanisms in conjunction with technological innovation will ensure infinite substitution possibilities capable of mitigating long-run physical resource scarcity.	A resource conservationist and 'managerial' position; infinite substitution is thought not realistic but sustainable growth is a practical option as long as certain resource management rules are followed.	A resource preservationist position: prior macroenvironmental constraints on economic growth are required because of physical and social limits: a decentralised socio-economic system is necessary for sustainability.	An extreme preservationist position supported by an acceptance of bio-ethics.

Source: R. Kerry Turner, 'Sustainable Global Futures', *Futures*, October 1987

Figure 3.8 The range of views from technocentrism to ecocentrism

The 1970s: The Limits to Growth

In 1972 *The Limits to Growth* was written as the outcome of meetings of the Club of Rome. This was a group of people who gathered to discuss the future of the world at a time of increasing environmental concern. It warned of a potential doomsday scenario for the year 2010 based on projections of future growth. The researchers who developed the scenario used a computer model to make their calculations.

The five major elements contributing to the impending global disaster are shown in Figure 3.9.

Figure 3.9 Limits to growth

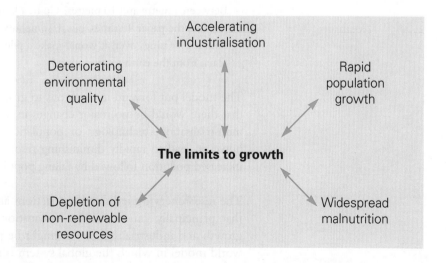

The model made the assumption that each of these five elements is changing at an accelerating rate known as exponential growth. The model was based on historical trends between 1930 and 1970 which are shown in Figure 3.10.

Figure 3.10 Growth trends

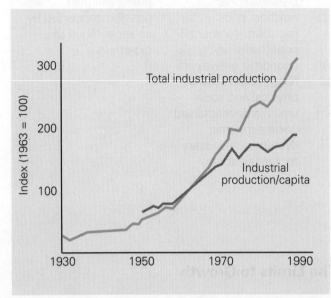

Index (1963 = 100)

300

200

100

Total industrial production

Industrial production/capita

1930   1950   1970   1990

Source: D. Meadows, et al., *Beyond the Limits*, Earthscan, 1992

The Law of Diminishing Returns alerts us to the fact that an absolute limit on one factor or element in the production process, will ultimately lead to diminution in the output achieved as a result of continued applications of other factors. If this were not so, if output increased in proportion to the total inputs of all factors, irrespective of the limit in supply of any one factor, it would be possible, with endless effort and much fertilizer, to produce unlimited supplies of, say, tomatoes from a window box. When expressed in this way, the argument seems to be self-evidently true. However, when the ultimate limit is considered on a global scale, the impact seems less easy to conceptualise, let alone identify and anticipate.

The central issue addressed in *The Limits to Growth* was: given the finite resources available on earth, what would be the effect of continued economic growth? One of the key features of their vision of growth was its exponential nature, which is explained as follows:

'Take a piece of paper and fold it in half. You've just doubled its thickness. Fold it in half again to make it 4 times its original thickness. Assuming you could go on folding the paper like that for a total of 40 times, how thick do you think it would get to be?' Less than a metre? Between a metre and 10 metres? Up to a kilometre? 'In fact you could not fold the paper 40 times, but if, somehow, its thickness could be doubled 40 times over, it would make a pile of paper high enough to reach from the earth to the moon.'

The model put forward in the limits to growth is based on the assumption that there would be no major changes in the supply of resources, levels of industrialisation, technology or population growth rates. Growth would however, lead to rapidly diminishing resources, reduced industrial output, increased pollution followed by falling population.

The researchers argued that if restrictions are placed on the two elements that principally cause resource exhaustion and pollution – population growth and industrialisation – it might be possible to achieve a stabilised world model in which the global system is in a state of equilibrium.

Limits to Growth: the conclusions

1 If the present growth trends in world population, industrialisation, pollution, food production and resource depletion continue unchanged, the limits to growth on this planet will be reached sometime within the next one hundred years. The most probable result will be a rather sudden and uncontrollable decline in both population and industrial capacity.

2 It is possible to alter these growth trends and to establish a condition of ecological and economic stability that is sustainable far into the future. The state of global equilibrium could be designed so that the basic material needs of each person on earth are satisfied and each person has an equal opportunity to realise their individual human potential.

3 If the world's people decide to strive for this second outcome rather than the first, the sooner they begin working to attain it, the greater will be their chances of success.

Source: Donella Meadows et al., *The Limits to Growth*, a report of the Club of Rome's project on the predicament of mankind, Earthscan, 1972

At the time of its publication, the book was subject to considerable criticism from technocentrist economists who believed that both technological change and substitution would avoid the Domesday scenario which had been painted. Malthus and others who made similar pronouncements in the past had been proved wrong. This did not mean that the problems could be ignored but that with careful stewardship, the planet would survive for longer than had been predicted.

Such publications do serve a purpose even if their message is regarded as extreme by many. They raise the profile of the issue, which is exactly what this one did. The environment had not been a significant feature on the international agenda until then.

Among the ideas which sprang from its thinking was steady state economics which can be summed up in the following passage from the book of the same name.

> Rich countries have wanted to place the burden of scarcity on the poor countries through population control. Poor counties have wanted to place the burden on the rich through limiting consumption. Both want to pass as much of the burden as possible on to the future.

> The simple solution is for the rich to cut consumption, the poor to cut population and to raise consumption to the same new reduced rich level and both to move towards a steady state at a common level of capital stock per person and stabilised or reduced population.

> The benefits of growth have not been distributed equitably on either a national or global scale. Today global communications systems and the mass media make these discrepancies glaringly obvious. The relatively poor are aware of their 'relative poverty'. – H. E. Daly, *Steady-state Economics: The Economics of Biophysical Equilibrium of Moral Growth*, W. H. Freeman, 1977

No-growth economics was the solution to the ecocentrists' view of the world. By using any more resources the world was in danger of meeting with dire consequences. This was the theme that ran through *Global 2000 Report to the President of The United States*, which re-ran many of the issues raised in *Limits to Growth*.

The technocentrists again attacked on the grounds that the empirical data was inaccurate and the problems were compounded when the erroneous data was fed into a computer model. The capitalist world was vehemently opposed to the *Limits to Growth* lobby because it demanded a no-growth scenario to overcome the problems which had been identified.

1980s–1990s: beyond the limits

During the 1980s, the debate shifted from concern about the physical limits because it became accepted by many that, in principle, the world's resources are sufficient to meet long-term human needs. The search for sustainable development became the focus of attention. The key factors involved were identified as:

- the uneven spread of population compared with the resources available;
- the inefficient and irrational use of natural resources;
- the interdependent nature of the problems which confront the world.

The migration of population in China, which was discussed in Enquiry 2 is exactly the type of issue which has become the focus of attention. Much of the 'irrational' use of resources comes about because people in poverty may have few options. In both Africa and India, many people rely on local supplies of timber for cooking and heating. As a result, trees have been destroyed which may in turn lead to soil erosion. This depletes agricultural potential and may leave areas uninhabitable.

Interdependency became a key feature of the change in thinking in the 80s.

The Brandt Reports of 1980 and 1983 stressed the importance of the sustainability of the international trading system. They advocated export-led growth as a means of advancement for developing countries. This policy was only successful for the few newly industrialised economies and would have been hard to achieve for most countries.

The Club of Rome's report stressed interdependency but was still concerned about the physical limits of the global system and worried that the speed of change was so rapid that there might not be time to react.

The Brundtland Report: Our Common Future, 1987 took the view that a new era of economic growth was feasible provided that it was based on policies that sustain and expand the environmental resource base. By doing this, the needs of the present can be met without compromising the needs of future generations.

The Pearce Report: Blueprint for a Green Economy, 1989 was originally written to provide advice for the Department of the Environment. It set out strategies for governments to deal with environmental issues through the market and provided methods of measuring the damage that was being done.

The Earth Summit, 1992 in Rio de Janeiro marked the first time that governments throughout the world had been drawn together to discuss the impact of growth and industrialisation on the environment. From it emerged targets and strategies for containing the damage.

Open Question

What type of problems will the market be unable to cope with?

The methods which have been advocated in *Blueprint for a Green Economy* have become the key to many governments' policies in the environmental field. Achieving sustainability by using the market to control wherever possible but resorting to targets and legislation where necessary has become the objective in the fields in which governments are currently trying to control the situation.

4 The national position

The UK is committed to meeting targets set by both international organisations and the EU for environmental protection. Europe's targets are often more stringent than those laid down by international organisations whose objectives tend to be broader.

The world context

The Earth Summit – or the United Nations Conference on Environment and Development – set out a programme to improve conditions in both these fields. As it aims at the next century it was entitled *Agenda 21*. The objective of improving the quality of life for many is not always purely environmental but the strategy of free trade, for example, may help to encourage developing countries to import new clean technology. The general acceptance of higher environmental standards will make legal measures more generally acceptable throughout the world. The objective of many points in *Agenda 21* is to assist in containing problems within the limits.

Other products of the Earth Summit were:

■ the *Climate Change Convention* which established a framework for action to limit the emission of greenhouse gases;
■ the *Biodiversity Convention* to protect species and habitats throughout the world;

■ a *Statement of Principles* for the management, conservation and sustainable development of the world's forests.

Agenda 21

Allocating international aid to programmes with high returns for poverty alleviation and environmental health, such as providing sanitation and clean water, reducing indoor air pollution and meeting basic needs.

Investing in research and development to reduce soil erosion and degradation and putting agricultural practices on a sustainable footing.

Allocating more resources to family planning and to primary and secondary education, especially for girls.

Supporting governments in their attempts to remove distortions and macro-economic imbalances that damage the environment.

Providing finance to protect natural habitat and bio-diversity.

Investing in research and development of non-carbon energy alternatives to respond to climate change.

Resisting protectionist pressures and ensuring that international markets for goods and services, including finance and technology remain open.

Source: World Bank, World Development Report, 1992

In January 1994, the UK government presented Action Plans in response to the Earth Summit proposals. The strategy for sustainable development looked at what this meant for the UK and identified likely pressure points in the foreseeable future. It proposed methods by which government, industry and individuals would or could contribute to sustainability.

The European context

The EU's agenda has developed since 1974 when the first action programme was implemented. It covered three broad areas:

■ the reduction or prevention of pollution;
■ general environmental improvement;
■ joint EU action in international organisations.

Since these were established, they have been extended steadily and there are now over three hundred pieces of legislation dealing with the environment. They cover water quality, air pollution, noise pollution and emissions from petrol and cars.

Figure 3.11 '169 letters' received by EU member governments in 1992

Country	No. of letters
Belgium	10
Denmark	4
France	12
Germany	16
Greece	14
Ireland	16
Italy	13
Luxembourg	10
Netherlands	3
Portugal	17
Spain	14
UK	14

Source: 10th Annual Report of the Commission to the European Parliament on the application of community law 1992, *The Official Journal*, Vol. 36 C233, August 1993

Product development

Apart from the obvious environmental objectives, these laws and targets are designed to create a level playing field for industry in Europe. If all countries have the same standards, no one country will be at an advantage because costs of production everywhere will be affected by the rules in the same way.

One way of comparing the degree to which individual countries conform to environmental standards is to look at the number of '169 letters' which are sent to the governments. These are sent when the European Commission suspects that there has been an infringement and are shown in Figure 3.11. The majority are sent when governments have failed to comply with the time limits set for the enactment of environmental legislation. Only about a quarter are for breaking environmental laws. Few of these actually reach the European Court of Justice as agreement is reached before proceedings are finally taken.

There is a much greater number of initial complaints to the EU but these figures are very misleading because environmental pressure groups use the European Commission as part of their campaigning process in some countries but not in others.

5 The role of the individual

The green consumer leapt to the fore in the UK in the late 1980s. Suddenly every company became aware of the need to meet the demands for products which did less harm to the environment. CFCs disappeared from aerosols, detergents lost their phosphates, timber had to come from forests which were replanted and paper had to have been recycled. A Green Shopping Day was organised to encourage the movement.

There were ironies in this because consumers cause many problems by their increasing demands as spending power rises. This was reflected in the No Shopping Day that Friends of the Earth threatened to run in order to raise the profile of their fundamental belief that saving the earth meant consuming less, not just differently.

Consumers are remarkably selective in their areas of concern. Little thought is given to the production process involved in the shoes they wear or the television they watch. Many such consumer goods have a considerable impact on the environment.

Industry has responded to environmental demands with new products and a lot of marketing hype which probably, in the long run, did more harm than good. The green consumer was identified as an individual with well above average earnings so many companies thought this was an excellent opportunity to sell premium green products at a higher price. Many were genuinely beneficial but others attempted to pull the wool over the consumers' eyes. Cleaning products which had never contained phosphates were suddenly announced to be 'phosphate free' and sold at a higher price.

Several companies benefited considerably from responding to this new demand. Ecover, a small firm which produces environmentally friendly detergents increased sales from almost £1m to £5m in a year. Varta's mercury and cadmium free batteries increased market share from 7% to 17% in six months.

In the 1990s, the movement lost its momentum. Green products started to vanish from the supermarket shelves. The change of attitude was attributed to a variety of causes:

- Consumers felt that they had been taken for a ride. The press was full of stories of over enthusiastic marketing and purchasers were starting to lose faith in the products in general, as a result.
- Consumers believed that the green products were not as effective as the traditional ones. They were initially prepared to sacrifice a few pence on a product but this ceased if it failed to do the job.
- The economy moved from boom to recession. People's attitude shifted from seeking environmentally sound products to looking for value for money. So products with a green premium had no place on the supermarket shelves.

Despite this change, the consumer movement has had a significant impact on our shopping habits. Aerosols have not returned to using CFCs, recycled paper is still a significant feature on the shelves and more and more waste products are being recycled.

Open Question

Will self-interest always get the better of firms and individuals?

The green premium is a problem because people seem prepared to pay more in times of economic strength but their enthusiasm wanes when they have to monitor their spending carefully.

If green products could become cheaper than dirty ones, the market would turn round rapidly. When the government announced differential tax rates on leaded and unleaded petrol, there was a rapid switch to unleaded. Such changes can only be brought about by governments.

Consumers alone are unlikely to bring about a revolution because their knowledge is very dependent upon items that have hit the headlines. The need is for a coherent policy which enables both individuals and companies to make decisions which benefit themselves and the environment.

Enquiry 4:   What is the role of the market?

Scope

In this Enquiry the functioning of the market in relation to environmental issues is explored. To what degree will the market alone assist in solving the problem of non-renewable resources? Will it exacerbate the problem? The market is a powerful tool and governments are learning to use it effectively in order to meet the requirements which are being laid down by international organisations.

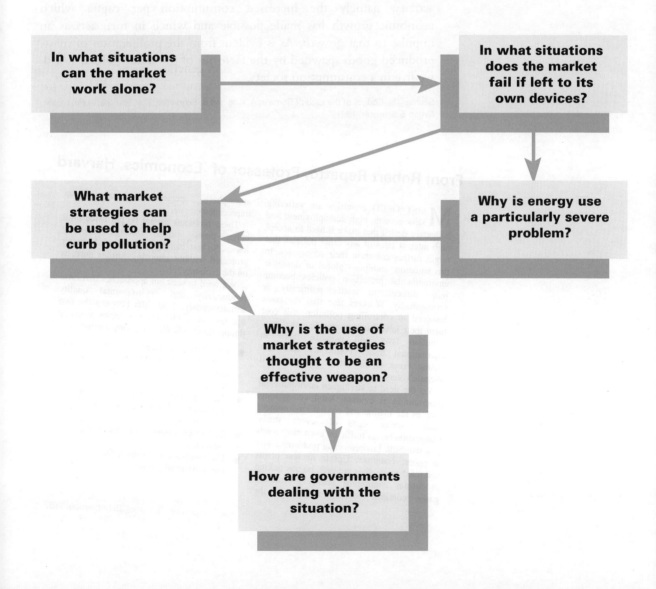

Opening evidence

From the Club of Rome

A central feature of the global situation is the enormous increase in the totality of human activity during the present century, which has led to a huge rise in the demand for raw materials and energy. Much of this increase is due to the spectacular growth of the world population during this period which will be added to in the years to come by cohort after cohort of new inhabitants to our planet …

… But there is an even more powerful factor in the growth of human activity, namely the increased consumption per capita which economic growth has made possible and which in turn acts as an impulse to that growth. As is evident from the proliferation of mass-produced goods spawned by the factories of the industrialised world, we live in a consumption society.

Source: The Council of the Club of Rome in A. King and B. Schneider, *The First Global Revolution*, Simon & Schuster, 1991

From Robert Repetto, Professor of Economics, Harvard

MOST OECD countries are suffering slow growth, high unemployment and budgetary deficit that make it hard to accept high interest rates or any other policies that might further constrain their economies. In this situation, ambitious global or domestic environmental protection policies become more difficult to justify politically or economically. Workers fear that the costs involved in controlling pollution will cost them their jobs. Businessmen fear that new pollution laws will penalise them in international trade. Politicians fear that raising taxes to discourage pollution will alienate voters.

Yet the need to strengthen environmental programmes is evident. Vital eco-systems such as the marine and coastal environment flash warning signs of severe stress. Congestion brings traffic on even more roads to a standstill. Environmental problems fester in poorer countries. Unsafe nuclear plants and toxic waste sites are time bombs ticking in former communist states, greenhouse gases continue to accumulate in the atmosphere, species disappear at an unprecedented rate.

These problems cannot be put aside until better times without risking staggering losses. So how can the environment be better protected without imposing further burdens on the economy?

We need to seek out approaches that raise productivity and environmental quality simultaneously. Trade offs between the two are not inevitable; many policies generate double dividends. Here are some examples:

- Lower income and profit taxes, and make up revenues through higher taxes on pollution, congestion and resources waste.
- Base environmental laws on market mechanisms that encourage efficiency and innovation.
- Reduce environmentally damaging subsidies.
- Use free trade as a vehicle for environmental progress.

Source: *Guardian*, 25 September 1992

From the European Union

FROM April 1995, voluntary Eco-Management and Audit Regulation (Ema) will be operating in all member states. It is designed to provide the public with credible data on a company's environmental performance, which can be compared with others across Europe.

To earn the coveted EU eco-audit label, a firm must first draw up a specific environmental improvement programme with clear targets, such as a pledge to cut energy use by 20% or improve its waste disposal. It will then carry out an internal audit to assess how well it is meeting its targets. After the audit has been verified by external specialists, the company may publish a report detailing its green performance.

Because it is voluntary, Ema will have to rely on market forces to persuade companies to sign up. The need to generate a clean public image has already encouraged some firms to produce green reports, although they vary from high quality to public relations blurb.

Source: *The European*, 1 April 1994

Industry and self interest

Since companies are not altruists, most will be only as green as governments compel them to be. They will do what is required of them and what they perceive to be in their own self interest. That is as it should be. It is not the job of companies to decide what values ought to be attached to natural resources and what the priorities of environmental policy ought to be, any more than it is their job to decide what share of national income should go into education and what the speed limit should be. The setting of environmental priorities and their translation into price signals and regulation is government's role.

Source: Frances Cairncross, *Costing the Earth*, Harvard Business School Press, 1992

From the fishermen

MORE than one hundred fishing vessels blockaded three of Scotland's busiest west coast ports to protest against government legislation designed to limit the number of days they can spend at sea.

The Sea Fish (Conservation) Act, which limits some fishermen to 80 days a year, is designed to help conserve fish stocks and to comply with an EU agreement to cut British capacity by 19%. Fishermen claim that a £25 million compensation scheme, two thirds funded by the EU is not enough.

John Henderson, skipper of The Crest, based at Mallaig, said 'I have spoken to no fisherman that agrees with this legislation. We see this as an evil law, on a par with the legislation that created the Highland clearances. It's going to put fishermen out of business.'

Source: *The Times*, 1 June 1992

1 Striving for success

Firms all work within the macroeconomy to produce a profit which is acceptable to their shareholders. To achieve this, a company must aim to influence either the demand or supply curve by testing and pushing at the limits which were identified in Enquiry 1.

Pushing out the limits without breaking the rules

FAIRY is a good example of 'runaway success'. Ten years ago its market share was less than 30%. Today it's 53% and climbing. Since Procter & Gamble relaunched the brand last August (as Fairy Excel), Lever's Persil, the second biggest brand has slumped six points to 12%. Colgate's Palmolive liquid has been withdrawn and supermarket own-label penetration has fallen. But Proctor & Gamble has done this not by breaking the rules but by keeping strictly to them.

Rule one: deliver demonstrable product benefit through superior technology. Fairy Excel's breakthrough was not the result of any special project but part of the continual programme of on-going research. Although marketers are always searching for new tricks, the consumer is always looking for value when it comes to washing dishes.

Rule two: ram the message home with high profile, straightforward television advertising. The cost of the campaign for Fairy Excel and, their dishwasher product, Glazeguard, will be £15 million.

Rule three: never depart from your brand values and stick with your advertising strategies and agencies. Nanette Newman has been advertising 'mild green Fairy Liquid' since 1981.

Source: Adapted from *The Times*, 20 October 1993

Cost structure

Procter and Gamble's success in increasing sales of its prime washing-up liquid demonstrates how the market can be used to a company's benefit. The demand curve for its product has been shifted substantially by an effective marketing campaign. This probably results in greater cost effectiveness as overheads or fixed costs will be spread over greater output, so profitability rises.

Apart from the firms with which Procter & Gamble competes, no one suffers from its activities. Consumers make the decision that this is the washing-up liquid that they want and Procter & Gamble is benefiting from its skill in selling the product. The environment may not have gained substantially, but its rivals' policy on this issue was probably little different, so the *status quo* still holds on that front.

There are many examples of firms using existing strategies and systems to push out the limits in order to increase output or profits, or introduce new products. Not all of them are as benign.

2 Why does it all go wrong?

How many fish are there in the sea?

Nearly 80% of all fish caught by European Union countries is taken in the traditional British waters of the North-East Atlantic. There is intense competition to catch fish among the fishing industries of many countries including Britain, Denmark, Spain and the Netherlands. The Danes, who specialise in scouring the sea to produce fishmeal, are the leading fishers in the EU at least by volume of catch followed by the Spanish with Britain and France vying for third place.

The Common Fishing Policy of the EU has established quotas for member states. This policy is a fine balancing act between conserving fish stocks and not bankrupting the boat owners.

The current method provides for a Total Allowable Catch (TAC) which is a set amount in tonnes that may be taken of key species such as cod, haddock, whiting, mackerel and herring. Each member state is given a quota from the total based on its traditional catch. The system however, encourages exhaustive fishing as each

boat tries to haul in as much as possible before the national quota is exhausted.

The growth of 'industrialised' fishing has added to the problem. Ever bigger trawlers with ever bigger nets have depleted the seas of cod, haddock, whiting, plaice, mackerel and herring. The destruction is intensified because sand eels and other small species upon which they feed are also being caught in their billions to be turned into fish-meal for intensively-reared pigs and poultry.

These fishing practices have led to immense waste because small, less valuable specimens are discarded to die because landing them would fill the quota. In 1991 more haddock was caught and discarded than landed. Quotas are also widely ignored. A report published by Greenpeace in June 1992 indicated that while 350,000 tonnes of cod were landed each year in the UK in the 1970s, today the figure is more like 60,000 tonnes because of depletion by overfishing.

Figure 4.1 Diminishing fish catches

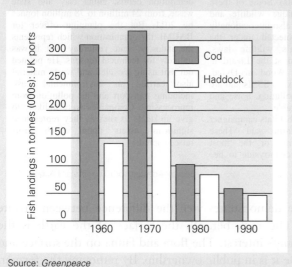

Source: Greenpeace

Figure 4.2 Disputed fishing grounds

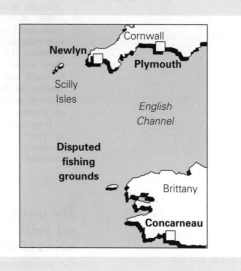

The fishing industry has existed ever since the human race discovered it as a source of food and it has always led to disputes. Rules have been made about boundaries and how many fish can be caught but dissent continues. How can you determine whose fish are whose?

This is the key question which exemplifies the core of the market failure problem. If ownership is clear, a resource will be looked after. If the supply is limited it will be conserved or alternatives will be sought. There are many examples of the search for alternatives to primary products. Oil, rubber and copper have all been the subject of such activity, with varying degrees of success. Anything which seems to belong to no one, however, will suffer from everyone's abuse.

Substitution

The air, rivers and seas have all suffered in the same way. Open access leads to problems.

Quarries for road building threaten wildlife havens

MORE than 100 wildlife havens are under threat from quarrying and mining to provide materials for road building and other construction.

The new study carried out by Friends of the Earth is based on planning rights which date from before the First World War but have been lodged over the last two years with local authorities. It shows that companies are claiming rights to develop quarries in some 70 Sites of Special Scientific Interest (SSSIs). Some of these SSSIs, areas with unique wildlife and geological features, are also internationally important habitats, protected under the European Commission's wildlife laws. They include heathland at the Lizard in Cornwall and Carmel Wood in Dyfed. Another 40 sites are next to SSSIs and are likely to suffer from pollution, noise and alterations to the water table.

Tony Juniper, senior habitats campaigner at Friends of the Earth, said 'These permissions allow some of the most treasured parts of our countryside to be wrecked … all interim development orders should be revoked and the wider implications of the national road programme reviewed.'

Recent government forecasts show that demand for minerals and aggregates will rise by 66% from 250 – 300 million tonnes to 500 million tonnes by 2011. The environment department has asked the industry if it is possible to increase the use of recycled or waste materials, such as demolition debris, china clay and slate waste, from 24 million to 78 million tonnes by 2011. But the planning officer for BACMI, the organisation which represents the industry, said yesterday that it was unlikely for technical reasons. He pointed out that using recycled and waste material also carried an environmental cost, including transport and air pollution from reprocessing. Companies were unlikely to give up rights to sites as they represented significant assets upon which firms raised capital.

Source: Adapted from *The Times,* 3 August 1993

The quarrying issue demonstrates well the difference between private and public goods. The rock beneath the surface of the earth is the subject of the company's interest. The flora and fauna on the surface and the atmosphere above it is in public ownership. By removing the former, the latter is damaged. In these circumstances, it is only by government action through legislation that the environment can be protected.

This explains why the problems of acid rain, polluted oceans, global warming and the thinning of the ozone layer are all issues that are so difficult to deal with. Because no one owns these resources, no one feels the need to look after them. By using them as a cheap dumping ground, firms can lower their costs and achieve private efficiency while causing social inefficiency.

Private costs and social costs

3 Can the market curb pollution?

Source: Carlucho in Mark Bryant (ed.), *Turn Over a New Leaf*, Earthscan, 1990

By identifying the source of the problem and its perpetrators, the market can be turned to good effect in the battle to control pollution. The *polluter pays principle* can be used to encourage those who create the mess to seek other, less harmful methods. There are a variety of strategies which can be employed to put this into practice.

Green taxes

Green taxes have been among the environmentalist's armoury since the 1920s when Arthur Pigou, the Cambridge economist, introduced the idea of using taxation to bridge the gap between private and social costs. They have however been used little since then. Many countries are now starting to employ them in their search for methods of controlling all sorts of environmentally damaging behaviour from the excess use of plastic bags to city centre traffic congestion.

The problem with green taxes is lack of information. Figure 4.3 shows the range of information required to fix such taxes accurately.

■ The firm's output of goods

■ The pollution dose which this output produces

■ Any long-term accumulation of pollution

■ Human exposure to pollution

■ The damage response of this exposure

■ The monetary valuation of the cost of pollution damage.

Source: David Pearce and Kerry Turner, *Economics of Natural Resources and the Environment*, Harvester Wheatsheaf, 1990

Figure 4.3 The necessary information

The difficulty is that not only are these hard to calculate but they may be subject to disagreement. Evaluating the damage caused by a particular dose of pollution is hard enough but the benefit value to society of the product from the factory must be known as well if an equilibrium point is to be found.

Difficulties also arise in government because the environment departments have different motives from those of finance ministries. The latter view the prospect of extra revenue with glee whereas the former want to see the revenue from the tax used to further environmental improvements. Companies, of course, dislike green taxes because they increase prices and make them less competitive. Such taxes have also been criticised for being regressive. They add to the costs of production or travel, and hit the poorer sectors of the community hardest.

The effectiveness of a pollution tax depends largely on the elasticity of demand for the end product. Figure 4.4 demonstrates the effects on two different products with different elasticities. In the diagrams, t is the amount of the tax, P_1-P_0 represents the amount of tax paid by the consumer and $P_0-(P_1-t)$ represents the amount of the tax that the producer must absorb.

Figure 4.4 Passing on a pollution tax

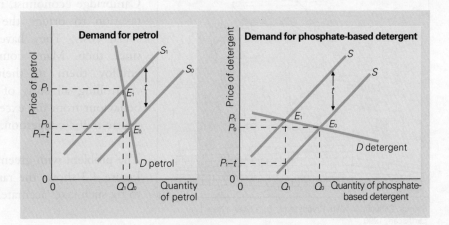

If demand is inelastic, the cost of the tax can be passed on to the consumer and there may be little change in sales. This occurs with petrol, because if car owners are to use their cars, there is no substitute for it. It will take a large increase in the tax to induce consumers to change their habits. If however, demand is elastic, consumers may save paying the tax by switching to a substitute, in this case a non-phosphate based detergent instead of the phosphate based one. The producer will not be able to pass on the tax, which will be highly effective in altering consumption patterns. This will force producers to reduce output of the environmentally unfriendly product.

Elasticity of demand

Tax incidence

The trick for the government is to set the tax at a point where it is cheaper to change habits than continue polluting. This is, of course, the most difficult part of the exercise: it is not easy to predict the most effective tax rate.

If pollution taxes are not to handicap the companies of any one country they must be universally accepted. Few countries will be willing to set up rigorous pollution control in isolation if it raises production costs and reduces competitiveness. The move towards international standards is therefore a necessary step to achieve significant change on this front.

Tradeable permits

The way they work

Tradeable permits use the market place to control the level of pollution. They set ceilings because a fixed number of permits, which represents a specific amount of pollution, is allocated to each polluter. They can then buy and sell them to each other if they have a shortage or surplus.

For them to work, a decision must be made as to how much pollution is acceptable. Permits are then issued to this level. As the system begins, too severe a cut back on emissions would lead to disruption so the amount that is initially acceptable often reflects a historic pattern. This system, known as grandfathering, is not the only way to begin but has proved the most acceptable to companies. It is, of course, important to achieve this acceptability at the inception of the programme.

The initial allocation will only improve the environment if it is at a lower level of pollution than has been experienced before or is setting the trend to reduce the level over time. A programme of reductions will, therefore, be necessary if the objectives are to be achieved.

Once the allocation has been made, any company which cuts emission levels to below the level of their permits can sell those they have left. So for a company which finds that the cost of cleaning up is less than the money that it can earn from selling the permits, there is a strong incentive to cut pollution. Other companies, whose costs are higher, will find that they welcome the opportunity to purchase the surplus permits from these companies. This is known as external trading. Internal trading may occur if a company finds that it has more than one source of pollution. The lower cost source may be able to create spare permits, by cheap abatement strategies, which it then trades for sources which are more difficult to solve.

In practice

In the US, where tradeable permits have been used since the 1970s, most trading has been internal. This appears to be caused by the expense of acquiring sufficient information to establish a market. Finding out how many credits other companies hold and at what price they are likely to sell, takes a great deal of time and therefore the costs are high. Uncertainty about the future also encourages firms to hold on to spare permits as they are credits for future use. Such hoarded permits are also a barrier against new entrants into an industry.

Issues

Environmentalists have argued that the idea of a permit to pollute is wrong and it should just cease but the functioning of the system has demonstrated that effective reductions have been made. Most green groups have now accepted and appreciate the merits of the process.

Industry, although it never welcomed the use of tradeable permits at least feels that it has a degree of certainty about future levels of emissions and can plan accordingly. The government's objective is to keep down the administrative costs. With a few polluters there is no problem. If the number is high, costs rise sharply.

The barriers to entry problem can become serious if it is used as a deliberate strategy. A company, or group of companies which buys up all available permits, puts themselves in a very strong monopoly position and the government would have to investigate if this started to occur.

Adapting the idea

In New Zealand tradeable permits have been used to overcome the problem of allocating fish to fishermen, a problem which seemed to be insoluble. The initial quotas were 'grandfathered' and then various strategies were introduced to cut the catch to the total amount allowable. The government bought back some of the quota at the full price and offered 80% of the price to anyone else who wanted to sell. The rest of the cuts were made pro rata across the remaining quotas. The fishing companies had to pay a royalty to the government for their quotas, a figure which was doubled for foreign boats.

The system appears to have worked smoothly and quotas are traded readily both privately and through brokers who act as intermediaries. Initial teething troubles have involved price instability and the perennial problem of any tradeable permit system, the attempt to corner the quota market. With careful monitoring these problems can be solved so the system provides a model for overcoming many resource allocation difficulties. The fishing industry feels more in control of its own destiny because of the possibility of buying more quotas and therefore increasing their allowable catch.

The success of tradeable permits comes from putting a 'price' on resources which have no ownership and so creating a market for them. It has been suggested that they might be used on an international basis to deal with whole countries' output of carbon dioxide. If the costs of reducing emissions are low in one country, they would be able to sell their spare permits to countries where costs of reduction were higher. At least an evaluation process would then have to be carried out by each country to decide what could be done.

4 Energy: a source of the problem?

The problem

The burning of fossil fuels is one of the most damaging of the human race's activities. It contributes to acid rain, global warming and health problems. There appears to be no source of energy that is totally benign. Hydro-electricity damages water courses as rivers generally need to be dammed, tidal power destroys estuaries and therefore harms the bird life and wind power is an eyesore wherever it is installed. Some of these costs are of course harder to evaluate than others and this compounds the problem.

Efficient allocation of resources

Energy is used inefficiently because the full costs of its use are never charged. The externalities mentioned above are generally ignored. Energy, or the use of cars, which amounts to the same thing, is often subsidised. In many European countries coal production is subsidised although by burning it, large additions are made to the carbon dioxide in the atmosphere. Figure 4.5 shows the source of carbon dioxide emissions in the UK and estimates of future trends.

Figure 4.5 Carbon dioxide emissions in the UK

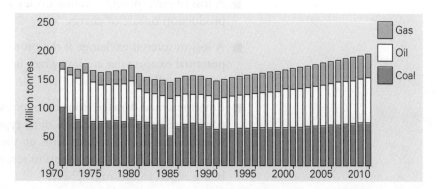

Source: Terry Barker (ed.), *Green Futures For Economic Growth*, Cambridge Econometrics, 1991

The effects

Demand and supply

If energy is under-priced, consumption will be higher than if it were sold at the market price. In Eastern Europe, energy prices were deliberately kept low to assist the development of industry and several countries became extremely intensive energy users. Figure 4.6 shows how these countries compare with others in the same 'lower middle income' category. They are not the only countries to subsidise energy. In Egypt, for example, energy prices were 20% of world averages and the World Bank had to encourage the government to raise them in order to reduce distortions. Industrial customers are still only paying 70% of the long run marginal cost of power.

Figure 4.6 Energy usage in Eastern Europe

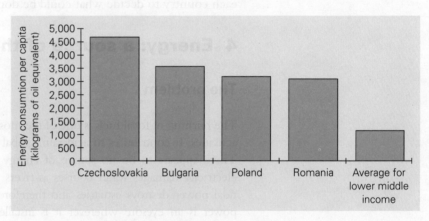

Source: World Bank, *World Development Report,* 1993

Many problems stem from the availability of cheap power. If demand is higher than the market equilibrium because the product is under priced there will be:

■ Incentives to develop energy intensive industry. These are often capital intensive and therefore inappropriate for developing countries with many poor people seeking work.

■ A loss of government revenue from paying subsidies on the production or sale of energy.

■ A loss of foreign exchange if the product has to be imported or if potential export sales are lost when home demand is above the market equilibrium.

■ Environmental damage from both excess production and consumption. The generation of all types of electricity has its costs, whether it is from building dams on the Amazon or wind mills on the Pennines. Excess consumption results in more carbon dioxide being added to the atmosphere.

Figure 4.7 gives an example of how the use of subsidies can distort the market and add to pollution. The top line on the graph shows the outcome of the increase in demand that would result if Poland continued on its 1988 path. The second line shows the effect of raising energy prices to US levels and the third line shows how pollution would fall with European prices.

Figure 4.7 The effect of energy prices on air pollution in Poland, 1988–2000

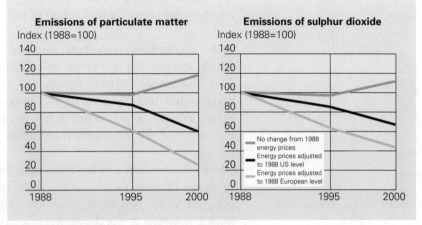

Source: World Bank, *World Development Report*, 1992

A market solution: the carbon tax

The market not only causes some of the environmental problems which we face but can be used to address them. By using taxation and other market based instruments, the government can attempt to create a situation in which marginal social cost is equal to marginal social benefit. This means that the consumer is paying a price equivalent to the full cost of the polluting product.

Elasticity of demand

A carbon tax, which is based on the carbon content of each fuel, would be an effective method of creating an incentive to use energy more efficiently. It could be used flexibly, which is important because the effects are uncertain and adjustments might need to be made, as follows:

■ By making it an *ad valorem* tax, which is based on a percentage of the price, the incentive effect would be greater because people would pay more, the more they use.

■ An escalating tax, which rose from one year to the next, would provide an incentive to adjust production methods or household heating. This process is slow and expensive so a yearly rise would be more equitable as it would give people warning of the future and time to adjust.

■ By taxing fuel use according to carbon content, people are persuaded to shift to less harmful fuels. Coal would therefore bear the highest rate, followed by oil, then gas.

Cambridge Econometrics, a consultancy organisation associated with Cambridge University, has used its computer model of the economy to assess the impact of such a tax. It posed two objectives: one to meet the UK aim of keeping emissions at 1990 levels and the other, to meet the international target set in Toronto of 80% of 1988 figures.

Some assumptions were built into the model, the most significant of which was that the tax would be compensated for by VAT adjustments. This means that inflation figures will not be affected and low energy users would actually gain. It also overcame one of the drawbacks of green taxation, which is that it hits the poor harder than the rich. The plan involved the introduction of the tax in 1991.

The tricky question is, what is the right level of tax? Assessing the amount to charge in order to achieve the point where marginal social cost equals marginal social benefit is extremely difficult. By using the computer model, however, it was discovered that to achieve the targets, the levels of taxation which are shown in Figure 4.8 would be required.

Figure 4.8 Targets and carbon taxes

	1991	1992	1993	2005
UK target	3.1	6.2	9.3	46.5
Toronto target	10	20	30	150

Source: Cambridge Econometrics

Because of the VAT compensation the overall effect on the economy of the carbon tax would be very slight. There would be a fall in employment in the coal industry but a rise in electricity and gas plus a rise in service industries as they would benefit from the fall in VAT.

The model was used to predict the effect of a package of green measures, including a tax on polluters and measures to improve water quality, on the economy as a whole. It identified how certain economic variables would differ, comparing the carbon tax scenario with that of continuing current policies (the base). The results are shown in Figure 4.9. Do not forget, however, that in using a model in this way, other macroeconomic trends will be picked up in the data.

'Whilst I would agree with you that we in the West must take drastic steps to reduce consumption of fossil fuels ...'

Source: Rupert Besley in Mark Bryant (ed.), *Turn Over a New Leaf*, Earthscan, 1990

Figure 4.9 The macro-economic effects

	1995	2000	2005
GDP and its components			
(% difference from base)			
Consumer expenditure	0.5	1.8	4.2
Fixed investment	1.4	2.1	2.7
Exports of goods and services	−0.1	−0.6	−1.2
Imports of goods and services	0.4	0.5	1.1
GDP at factor cost	0.4	0.9	2.2
Inflation			
(percentage point different from base)			
Consumer prices	0.1	0.3	0.1
Average earnings	0.3	0.6	0.7
Balance of payments			
(percentage point different from base)			
As a % of GDP	−0.2	−0.5	−1.1
Employment			
(different from base on '000s)			
Employment	191	427	682
Unemployment	−92	−207	−365

Source: Cambridge Econometrics

Figure 4.10 The reduction in energy intensity

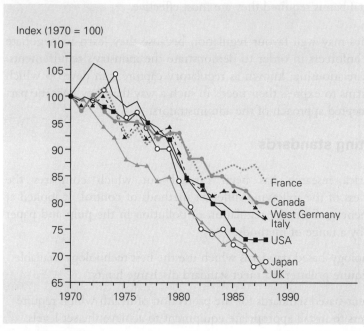

Source: OECD, 1991

The objective of such a tax would be to decouple the relationship between economic growth and energy use. The trend towards a reduction in the amount of energy used to produce £1 of GDP is already well under way as Figure 4.10 shows. All OECD countries have achieved a considerable reduction in the twenty years from 1970 to 1990. However, almost all countries' total energy use has continued to grow as their GDP has grown. Only Denmark has demonstrated this decoupling process as it succeeded in cutting energy use compared to its growth in GDP. In this twenty-year period, its GDP grew by 48% while total energy use actually fell a little.

5 Command and control

Regulations and targets

The market is not always the solution to controlling environmental damage. In fact, as yet, it has not been the solution that has been favoured by governments. Most environmental legislation relates to setting standards, or regulatory instruments.

Throughout Europe such standards are being set for all types of pollution. The newspapers frequently report the UK's standing in measures of drinking water, bathing water and many other indicators.

Open Question

Why is the market more efficient than regulation?

Although there is evidence that using the market is a more efficient method of keeping pollution, for example, in check, administrators prefer to work with targets and standards.

There are several reasons for this:

■ They require less information to work effectively than market instruments.

■ They can be depended on to achieve the intended target.

■ They are readily accepted politically because of the political and administrative support they generate.

■ If a total ban is required they are most effective.

Companies may well favour regulation because they learn to negotiate with the enforcers in order to demonstrate the industry's requirements. A special relationship, known as regulatory capture, can develop which enables firms to express their needs in such a way that they become part of the accepted approach of the administrators.

Evaluating standards

In America research has been carried out which compares the effectiveness of the following different methods of control. It looked at the net benefits from the regulation of pollution in the pulp and paper industry by a range of methods:

■ Technology-based standards which use the best technology available and require polluters to meet standard discharge limits.

■ Ambient-based standards for the protection of health which require polluters to install appropriate equipment to achieve the set levels.

■ Benefit-based standards which require polluters to install equipment which provides a balance between pollution reduction and the cost of pollution control.

Figure 4.11 shows the outcomes of the exercise. The technology based standard proved to be the least effective. Only 11 out of the 68 mills surveyed showed any benefit compared with 22 out of 60 with ambient based standards and 29 out of 60 with benefits based standards. The last two are regarded as more successful because they do not require ongoing monitoring of environmental standards. It also suggested that national standards may be inefficient because they may not be able to cope with local conditions. If market based methods were used, they would respond to such needs as they are less rigid.

Figure 4.11 The effectiveness of different methods of pollution regulation in the pulp and paper industry

Type of standard	Total benefits	Total costs	Net benefits
Technology	$36.6	$96.6	$–60.0
Ambient	$25.2	$23.8	$1.4
Benefits	$86.9	$55.8	$31.1

Source: R.A. Luken and L. Clark, 'How Efficient are National Environmental Standards? A Cost Benefit Analysis of the United States Experience', *Environmental and Resource Economics* 1, 1991

There are however arguments that market based measures 'crowd out' existing environmental ethics. This means that people abide by the market based rules and feel, as a result, that these actions absolve them from further responsibility for their actions. Regulation on the other hand, comes with social pressures to conform to a system which is publicly expressed to be beneficial.

Regulation and uncertainty

The effect of regulation can be uncertain because, as the time draws close for products to be banned completely, pressure groups spring up which want to lengthen the adjustment period. The requirement of the installation of catalytic converters in cars, for example, was delayed because manufacturers had stock piles of cars without converters, because sales had been depressed during a period of recession.

The case study 'Ozone friendlier' shows how those who plan to abide by the rulings may find themselves losing out as regulatory capture takes place and others cheat. It also points out that a tax on CFCs might have been a more effective method of dealing with the problem because everyone would then have had an incentive to seek alternative strategies instead of ignoring the problem.

Regulatory capture

Open Question

Is a tax which is approximately right better than the alternative solutions?

Ozone friendlier

DUPONT, the American chemical company has the dubious distinction of being the world's largest producer of CFCs. The firm had intended to stop making them for use in industrial countries by the end of 1994 but America's Environmental Protection Agency asked the company to continue in 1995.

This curious step has been noted nervously by some of Europe's chemical companies. Those, like Dupont, which have developed expensive substitutes for CFCs, long for CFCs to be banned from the market. Under an international agreement all industrialised countries were supposed to reduce the use of CFCs progressively until their use ceases in 1996. The EU has gone a step further so that from the start of 1995 the use of CFCs in Europe will virtually stop.

Like Dupont, some European producers have been busy shutting down their capacity for making CFCs. But they increasingly worry that some CFC users have done nothing to reduce their consumption, and instead seem to be playing a game of 'chicken' with governments.

Some users, it is true, have chopped their demand. Total use in Europe has fallen to within the regulation level. But the decline came almost entirely from aerosols and foam blowing. The demand from the refrigeration and air-conditioning industries has remained stubbornly constant.

The trouble is, the industries which use CFCs as a coolant are large and fragmented. They include transport companies, corner shops and building contractors. Reclaiming used CFCs has barely begun. In Britain, the Refrigerant Users' Group has surveyed its members to find out what they plan to do about the coming ban: some, apparently, do not know that they have CFCs in their fridges and air conditioners.

The best reminder would be a sharp rise in the price of CFCs. But in Europe their price fell last year; despite a slight rise since, the main CFC used as a coolant is still cheaper than the chief substitute, called 134A. Some less virtuous European producers are rumoured to be still running plants at full blast; another culprit may be the several thousand tonnes imported from Russia, supposedly to be cleaned up and returned, which is said to have found its way illicitly on to the European market. The real blame falls on European governments for not taxing CFCs as America does.

Significantly, in America, the EPA's concern with Dupont was that it might leave America's 140 million or so air conditioned vehicles without CFCs. Car makers have found it difficult to produce simple and reliable ways to refit old coolant systems with substitutes and there is probably not enough of the chemical banked away to supply the motorists when the ban starts.

Source: Adapted from *The Economist,* 29 January 1994

6 Markets, governments and the environment

Source: Stan Eales in Mark Bryant (ed.), *Turn Over a New Leaf*, Earthscan, 1990

The objectives of governments determine their actions with regard to the environment. They are, of course, working within the constraints laid down by organisations such as the EU which has a broader authority to set international standards.

The UK government has used the market, through taxation on fuel, to achieve the standards which have been laid down by the EU and other international bodies. When taxes are increased, the price rises and quantity demanded falls according to the degree of elasticity. As the demand for petrol is relatively inelastic, the result will be a considerable increase in tax revenue and quite a small fall in demand. This also provides a not insignificant boost to the government's spending power.

Figure 4.12 Petrol prices around the world

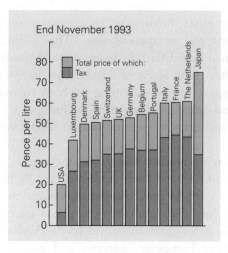

End November 1993

Pence per litre

Total price of which:
Tax

USA, Luxembourg, Denmark, Spain, Switzerland, UK, Germany, Belgium, Portugal, Italy, France, The Netherlands, Japan

Source: Opel

The graph in Figure 4.12 shows the UK's position on petrol prices and taxation, in relation to other countries. The US and Japan stand out as extremes but for different reasons. In the US petrol taxes are extremely low and in Japan, the pre-tax cost of the fuel is extremely high. Petrol tax is a political hot potato in the US and therefore a difficult one to increase substantially without suffering at the polls.

Although governments generally accept their stewardship of the environment and the resulting need to intervene, they also cause environmental damage by some of their own activities. People's attitudes to this damage will vary according to the value judgements that they hold on such issues. New road building will speed someone happily on the way to work, while others will condemn it for tearing up the countryside.

A greenish tinge

THE chancellor of the exchequer seems an improbable environmentalist. But his budget will allow Britain to sign the treaty on global warming, signed at Rio de Janiero, last year, which said that emissions of carbon dioxide in 2000 must be no higher than in 1990. It will cut a further one million tonnes of carbon off what Britain is expected to produce by the end of the century. All told, the government has done enough to reduce carbon output in 2000 by a fairly respectable 10 million tonnes, or 6% below what it would otherwise have been.

The three main carbon cutting measures in the budget are a 3p a litre increase in road fuel duties; a commitment to increase these duties by at least 5% in real terms in future budgets, and in time, electronic road pricing to finance motorways. A few extra grams of carbon will doubtless be saved by the doubling of grants for home insulation.

As with the chancellor's handout to help the poor and elderly pay for value added tax on domestic fuel, the government has learnt a belated lesson: if green taxes are to be politically acceptable, some of the proceeds need to be recycled in help for the poor.

Source: *The Economist*, 4 December 1993

In other fields, the economic sense of subsidising agriculture for example is questionable. The Common Agricultural Policy has encouraged farmers to produce as much as possible irrespective of the effect high levels of fertiliser use have on both the land and the water supply. Intensive farming has been encouraged and has affected the flora and fauna in many parts of Europe. Chalk downland is ploughed up, marshlands are drained and the species which depend on them disappear.

Market distortions

Having reached this point, the market can then not absorb all that is produced and farmers are directed by the EU's Set-Aside Policy to cut back production, turning the countryside into golf courses or leaving it to run wild. Remaining surpluses are exported with a subsidy to bring the price down to world levels. Agriculture is a political minefield in many European countries and governments have been unwilling to stand up to the powerful lobbying groups which rise against any change. The General Agreement on Tariffs and Trade is coming to their defence with demands for a reduction in the EU's common external tariff and reduced export subsidies.

The downfall of the centrally planned economies and their increasing desire to function within the market economy has lead to an opening up of the issue of their environmental problems.

As these countries move towards the market and seek acceptance in the international groupings such as the EU, their policies have to change. For east Germany this has been easier because reunification has provided resources to assist the process. Even so it has been uncomfortable and distressing for many whose jobs have disappeared as their output became unacceptable in the European context. The closing down of many of the lignite mines in Saxony provides an example of this change.

Structural change

A change of power

EASTERN Germany used to be almost entirely dependent on brown coal or lignite for its energy needs and in the former communist state miners held a position of special importance, enjoying a degree of ideological veneration.

Now the mining industry faces virtual bankruptcy. Thousands of miners will be laid off, mining towns will be emptied and electricity supplied through a unified German grid using cleaner western German hard coal or other energy sources.

From a maximum of 130,000 miners producing 300 million tonnes of brown coal, a maximum of 30,000 will be employed by the end of the decade. The number of active mines has fallen from 40 to 15 and output has been cut to a third.

Mining in East Germany was dirty, primitive and unhealthy for miners and the environment. The huge open cast mines and slag heaps still scar the landscape and clean up operations will cost billions. Restoring the landscape may soon be the main source of employment for laid-off miners.

Extraction machinery was primitive and the power generation plants inefficient and polluting. The acrid smell of brown coal smoke used to hang all over eastern German towns and the pollution was amongst the worst in Europe. Smog, lung disease and a constant film of grey dust on all streets and open surfaces characterised mining towns.

The miners were proud of their jobs, and have fought to prevent the death of their close knit communities, with marches, petitions and demonstrations. Mining towns in the east, as in Britain, were old communities, founded at the start of the industrial revolution. In the former East Germany, where state investment was at a standstill, many looked much as they had done before the second world war.

Only now is the damage inflicted by the coal industry in eastern Germany becoming apparent. For example, in Gorlitz, Saxony, the air contains 474 milligrams of sulphur monoxide per cubic metre, more than twice the permitted maximum. In future, east and west will rely more on natural gas.

Source: *The Times*, 27 January 1993

The environmental damage which has been caused by governments and companies across the political spectrum has now become the focus of world interest. The market has played a role in both its cause and its cure. The last section has shown that the market is by no means the worst offender and some of its shortcomings can be put down to ignorance: hindsight can provide great wisdom.

With careful stewardship, damage can be repaired and the limits which are currently perceived may become less finite.

7 Who's cleaning up?

Much of industry complains bitterly at the prospect of more stringent environmental rulings. The complaints generally focus on the additional costs involved and the effect that this will have on prices. There are, however, some companies which have treated the growing environmental movement as an opportunity to expand and develop markets which were originally opened up in the US.

Strategic planning

Open Question

How do some businesses succeed in taking advantage of these opportunities?

Regulations concerning emissions from power stations result in a growing market for increasingly sophisticated filters as the limits grow tighter. Control of sewage means rising demand for treatment works. All this means new business for those who are planning ahead.

The article below explains that the market in western Europe is worth $94 billion and will grow rapidly. As more countries become part of the EU, demand will be increased because most of the new entrants are significantly behind the rest on environmental issues.

The money in Europe's muck

DOES greenery damage your health? Many European companies, especially at the grubbier ends of manufacturing, complain about increasingly strict environmental controls. But one firm's expensive obligation is another's chance for profit. According to the Environmental Business Journal, based in San Diego, the market in Western Europe for environmental goods and services was worth some $94 billion last year – only $40 billion less than the market in America. The journal reckons that Europe's environmental industry is growing by 7% a year.

Ecotec, a British consultancy reckons that there are nearly 16,000 environmental firms in Europe. Many are small: 55% have annual sales of less than $2.5m. But Europe also attracts bigger players. Since 1989 the European subsidiary of America's Waste Management has almost quadrupled its annual turnover, to over $1.2 billion.

In environmental terms, Germany is Europe's California. Its laws are the toughest (and sometimes craziest) and its market for environmental goods and services is Europe's largest. Just as yesterday's Californian regulations have become today's federal law, so Germany's environmental laws often end up as EU policy.

Klaus Töpfer, Germany's robust environment minister, argues that tough standards have benefited German companies. He recalls that a decade ago he proposed tighter German standards for nitrogen oxides, to be told by protesting German industrialists that they were unattainable. Then Mr Töpfer discovered that they were already being achieved by companies in Japan. At first, German firms imported Japanese know-how; now, claims Mr Töpfer, Germany exports the technology, and its industry has become more energy-efficient.

Germany's environment agency (the UBA) reckons that the country spends 1.55% of its GDP on environmental investment – more than any other big industrial country. Germany is also, the UBA calculates, the world's leading exporter of environmental technology, with sales of DM35 billion ($22 billion) in 1992. That gave it 21% of the world export market, compared with America's 16%. Every time the EU adopts a German sponsored green law it creates more export opportunity for Germany's environmental firms and for their rivals elsewhere in Europe.

Take the market for municipal and industrial waste-water treatment. It has been hugely boosted by a European directive that will force Europe's big towns to have sewage-treatment plants by 2000; and its small towns by 2005. Given the primitive state of sewage treatment in some parts of Europe, that means lots of orders for new plants. Similarly, a European agreement to stop dumping sewage sludge at sea may, surprisingly, help Wessex Water, a British water company that used to be a big sea dumper. With the help of a Swiss firm called Combi, it now pasteurises its sewage and sells it as fertiliser.

The three giants of the French water industry – Générale des Eaux, Lyonnaise des Eaux Dumez and Bouygues's subsidiary, Saur – have been particularly successful at expanding abroad. One reason for their success it that they provide public authorities with a one-stop shop: they finance, build, and operate water-treatment plants. As a result, they have even broken into the German market.

Source: *The Economist*, 20 November 1993

The world market has grown steadily and forecasts for the future show a significant increase. Germany has the largest part of the environmental market in Europe but Britain has attracted a substantial slice as Figure 4.13 on p. 94 shows. The segments of the market are shown in the bottom section. Waste and water are the largest and have provided lucrative contracts throughout Europe. The other major sector of the market is for consultancy because as the laws change, companies are constantly seeking advice on how they should meet the requirements.

*Figure 4.13 The world
environmental market*

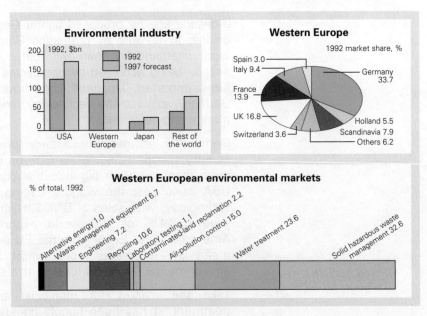

Source: Environmental Business Journal

Germany has generally led the demand for higher standards. In recent years, however, it has demonstrated less determination to tighten up because of the costs of reunification. Despite this, the European industry is probably on a sound footing because once European standards are being set, the trend for the future is in place and existing laws will keep the growing companies in business for a long time.

Enquiry 5:   Are the limits insuperable?

Scope

In the long term, unless firms and economies develop strategies which take account of the constraints, the limits will be met. In this Enquiry, existing strategy is explored and future possibilities which allow the limits to be surpassed are introduced. There is a vast range of ideas which may enable life to be different in future, but identifying the significant ones is a major task for shrewd entrepreneurs and wise governments.

Why has the Malthusian vision not yet come to fruition?

How is industry developing strategies to survive and expand?

How sustainable is growth in the UK?

Do these strategies assist in developing a sustainable economy?

What is being done to increase sustainability?

What trends exist that assist the achievement of sustainability?

What should firms and governments do in future to increase the degree of sustainability?

Opening evidence

From the future

IMAGINE sitting in a cardboard box at Wimbledon, watching the tennis through a hole cut in the side. That is effectively what TV is today. Imagine now that the TV screen is as big as the living room wall and gives you an unrestricted view; that there is a zoom facility which means that you become the camera man, controlling everything you see and hear.

Alternatively, you don a pair of virtual reality spectacles and are simultaneously transported to a specific seat in the Albert Hall or Yankee Stadium. As you move your head you see people around you. Your seat could simultaneously be occupied by hundreds, thousands or millions of people. We could all attend the Olympics without leaving home. It may sound far-fetched but the base technologies required for this and a vast range of equally futuristic developments are already available in research labs and the broadcast capacity is in place now.

Source: *The Times*, 12 September 1993

On the zero emission vehicle

The zero emission vehicle is no longer a figment of the imagination. It is being developed in Vancouver by Ballard Power Systems. Daimler Benz, Mazda and General Motors are all interested.

The fuel cell, which powers it, combines hydrogen and oxygen to release electricity and water. The idea is not new but, for the first time, a practical version has been produced.

A 40-foot vehicle with a range of 175 miles and capable of carrying 40 passengers is under development. None of the inputs to the fuel cell are burnt so there are no emissions. No parts of the power cells move so maintenance is reduced. They are modular in form so they can be added or removed with ease.

The whole design process aims to produce a vehicle which meets the market's requirements for both costs and usability. This is not just a scientist's toy but a product which combines potential profitability with environmental necessity.

From Stuart Willis, Overseas Director, Oxfam

SELDOM have the development policies espoused by northern governments promised so much. From Agenda 21, the Earth Summit blueprint for sustainable development, to the World Bank's promise of a 'sustained assault on world poverty', the message has been that the rich world must act to break the spiral of deprivation and environmental degradation in which the world's poorest countries are trapped.

But the rhetoric has served only to highlight a widening gulf between principle and practice. While industrialised countries preach the virtue of a new world order, their financial policies are even now widening the gap between rich and poor countries, and deepening the already abject poverty and environmental degradation in which more than a billion people live.

Source: *Guardian*, 25 September 1992

From Gro Harlem Brundtland, author of the Brundtland Report

The future of our children depends on our ability to learn to live in harmony with nature and each other. Sustainable development means that we cannot continue to satisfy our own needs at the expense of those of future generations.

All over the world there is a growing sense of urgency that radical steps are needed to reverse present negative trends. People are more and more worried about the deterioration of their natural and social environment. We see rapidly increasing pressure on those who have political responsibility to act quickly and forcefully.

Developments in Europe illustrate reasons to be optimistic. The European nations have confirmed that security can no longer be defined in military terms alone. We must establish a concept of security which can deal with the threats from poverty and environmental degradation at the same level of attention as has been given to the danger of war.

Source: Jonathon Porritt, *Save the Earth*, Dorling Kindersley, 1991

Can we have our cake and eat it?

No longer need industrial advance cause environmental degradation. We can have sustainable development instead; everyone can be both rich and green.

Yet environmentalists point out, the conflict remains. Environmental protection does mean constraints on economic activity. Although economic growth and conservation are not incompatible, they remain uneasy companions. There is surely a grave danger in glossing over their differences: the risk that, whatever the motive of its originators, sustainable development will effectively provide a green cover for 'business as usual'. By failing to specify exactly what degree of environmental protection is required, Greens warn, the term offers governments and industry a means of embracing environmentalism without commitment. The British government's officially published response to the Brundtland Report serves as a salutary illustration: a document wholly in favour of sustainable development which argues that British economic policy already conforms to it.

Source: Michael Jacobs, *The Green Economy*, Pluto Press, 1991

1   A pessimist's view and its downfall

Thomas Malthus viewed the problem of population as insuperable. In his *Essay on the Principle of Population as it Affects the Future Improvement of Society*, written in 1798, he said that society would crumble because there was a tendency in nature to outstrip all possible means of subsistence. The human urge to reproduce would result in poverty and starvation and would therefore lead to humanity destroying itself. However hard the human race worked, they would be unable to produce sufficient food to meet the needs of this ever-hungry population.

His thinking was based on the assumption that the population would double every 25 years, which was quite reasonable for his time. In America, this had happened for the previous 150 years. His only solution was 'moral restraint' which seemed unlikely to be a successful strategy in an age when many families ran into double figures.

Malthus' view was widely accepted by economists and the general public alike and has continued to influence thinking for nearly two centuries. The Club of Rome's pessimistic outlook, which was forged when the world's population was expected to increase five-fold, draws on the idea that natural resources will run out, making the future extremely uncertain. As yet these prognostications have not come to fruition. Why not?

Technological change, particularly in agriculture, has had a significant impact. Agriculture in the developed world has increased yields beyond Malthus' comprehension. This has been followed by the Green Revolution in a number of countries, such as India, which has enabled much of the developing world to produce sufficient to feed their people. There may still be a distribution problem, but the level of output has largely ceased to be an issue. There are, of course, crises when droughts and floods destroy the harvest but these are localised events and not empirical evidence for Malthus' fears.

Population growth is still a threat because the survival rate is rising in many developing countries. In many countries population is still growing at an alarming rate as the standard of living improves. The flood to the cities which was discussed in an earlier enquiry will continue to grow as rural populations seek the life style of the developed world.

However, by looking at general trends, it seems that there is hope on this front too. Soon after the Club of Rome had published its first report in 1972, the rate of growth of world population fell for the first time in history. It is now expected to level off in the first half of the next century – a change of direction which Malthus would never have dreamed of. This has resulted from the changing social structures as people have become

Structure of population

more urbanised. Children on the farm are an asset as they can always be found work and they will support their parents in old age. But in the city a large family is more of a liability. The improving survival rate for children means that there is less need to produce as many and the growing awareness and effectiveness of contraception has also helped to change the trend.

Forecasting

There are obvious dangers in making firm predictions about the future and it is very easy to condemn them as foolish when we have the benefit of hindsight. Malthus projected trends that he was witnessing and drew reasonable conclusions. Little did he know how much the world would change. Fortunately for us, the changes that have occurred make the objective of sustainable development more achievable than Malthus could have imagined.

Pushing beyond the limits to growth involves developments in several directions. They include:

■ stewardship of the resources that are currently available;
■ seeking technological change which allows us to use these resources more effectively;
■ seeking technological change which substitutes alternatives for the resources we currently use.

2 Moving towards sustainability

The stages to sustainability

The route to the achievement of sustainable development has been defined as having three stages, as shown in Figure 5.1. It involves not just political tinkering but a shift in both economic and social attitudes. The process is long and slow as cultural change is required.

Figure 5.1 The stages to sustainability

Stage	Policy	Economy	Social	Discourse
1 Ultra weak sustainability	Lip service to policy integration	Minor tinkering with economic instruments	Dim awareness and little media coverage	Corporatist discussion groups; consultation exercises
2 Weak sustainability	Formal policy integration and deliverable targets	Substantial restructuring of microeconomic incentives	Wider public education for future visions	Round tables; stake holder groups; Parliamentary surveillance
3 Strong sustainability	Binding policy integration and strong international agreements	Full economic valuation; green accounts at business and national level; green taxes	Curriculum integration; local initiatives as part of community growth	Community involvement; twinning of initiatives in the developed and developing worlds

Source: David Pearce, R. Kerry Turner, Timothy O'Riordan, *Blueprint 3*, Earthscan, 1993

Institutional problems in the UK

In the UK the government has never had an integrated policy on the environment. The fact that government structures do not lend themselves to such integration is a primary cause. The pattern of government, which has been long established, does not assist in the achievement of sustainability. The features which impede the process are the result of the evolutionary process which has created government ministries with strong areas of individual interest. The Department of Transport's main interest is in building roads and the Ministry of Agriculture, Fisheries and Food has concentrated on increasing output. Both ministries can be in direct conflict with the Department of the Environment.

Government policy tends to emerge from the ministries and other interested bodies, rather than from the prime minister and cabinet. As a result it may reflect a range of vested interests rather than the broader interests of the country. For policy to be properly implemented, the support of these ministries is required, so it is difficult for any party to develop effective legislation that over-rides these interests.

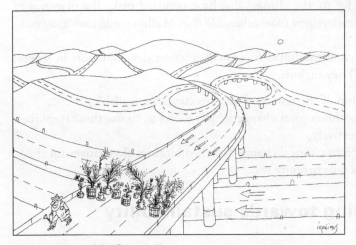

Source: Ironimus in Mark Bryant (ed.),
Turn Over a New Leaf, Earthscan, 1990

Policy integration

The Department of the Environment (DoE) is the lead agency for the UK's environmental policy but it does not have authority over all the areas which are involved in the process of achieving sustainability. As decision making is not co-ordinated and the interests of other ministries and pressure groups can influence factors which affect the environment, the development of an effective strategy is difficult to achieve. The case study, which explains why there is no policy on the extraction of aggregates, demonstrates the problem.

Policy failure: aggregates

Aggregates (i.e. sand, gravel and crushed rock) are required for building and road construction. What would a sustainable strategy for aggregates look like? At present about 15% are reused in road beds or building foundations; the rest is disposed of. The demand for aggregates is projected in terms of economic growth rates; indeed it is almost assumed that the need for fresh aggregates is the sign of a healthy economy, rather as energy growth was visualised in the 1970s. In 1991, the DoE estimated that demand for construction aggregates would rise from 300 million tonnes in 1989 to 505 million tonnes in 2011; a rise of 2% per annum. This raises two very important questions.

First, where would all this material come from? As the scope for winning aggregates in southern England or off the coast is reduced due to local protest and the need to nourish beaches, fresh aggregates are being sought from the hard rock 'peripheries', notably the outer Scottish islands. If Scottish super quarries create jobs and provide a restoration bond (which will not compensate for the loss of regional amenity and wildlife), is this socially and environmentally acceptable? The answer may be yes on very weak sustainability grounds but less clear on stronger sustainability grounds.

Second, which department would put in place a sustainable policy on aggregates? The DoE really only handles planning and it comes in at a relatively late stage in the policy process. The demand-led modelling is rooted in the Departments of Transport and Trade and Industry. Any attempt at amenity policy would have to pass through these two departments as well as the Treasury, which would be very unwilling to see any earmarking of funds for compensation or restoration. Any coherent policy on aggregates would have to connect demand reduction, recycling, planning betterment and pricing in a highly sophisticated manner: not easy.

Source: David Pearce, R. Kerry Turner, Timothy O'Riordan, *Blueprint 3*, Earthscan, 1993

The future

The government has made some attempts to overcome these problems and raise the awareness of the various ministries about their environmental responsibilities. It is difficult to judge the efficacy of these measures because much of the resulting work depends on internal liaison.

A range of environmental targets is in place in the UK. These are thought by some to be too limited both in their range and scope. Others view them more favourably because achievable targets are more likely to be successful. Some countries are happy to set excessively stringent targets, which receive a positive response from the world's environmentalists but are not unduly worried if they are never met. Reporting procedures on targets exist in the UK but the results are not always easy to interpret.

The government's response to Agenda 21, which was discussed in an earlier Enquiry has helped in setting out the policy for the future. As yet, the UK is scarcely at Stage 1 of the process of transition to sustainable development but it has made some progress in this direction.

Testing sustainability in the UK

If an economy is to be sustainable, it must be using resources at a rate which will allow future generations the same level of well-being. To achieve this it is important to know whether present consumption is greater than sustainable consumption. An index of sustainability has been developed, which is based on the idea that saving should be at least equal to the amount of depreciation on manufactured and natural capital.

In the following equation:

S   = gross national saving

$Detr.K_m$ = deterioration of manufactured capital

$Dep. K_N$ = depletion of natural capital

$Deg. K_N$ = degradation of natural capital

If

$$S = Detr.K_m - Dep. K_N - Deg. K_N,$$

the economy is just achieving sustainability. If S is greater, gains are being made and if S is smaller, the economy is not demonstrating sustainability.

This measure is for weak sustainability in which replacement is taking place but renewable capital is replacing non-renewable capital. This allows the economy to continue growing but may be causing depletion which is not recoverable. It also ignores changes in the size of population and technological advance.

The acceptable flexibility between renewable and non-renewable resources may not always be a reasonable solution. If some resources are *critical* to future development, their record must be looked at separately because any depletion would contribute more than proportionately to unsustainability. Even if the reduction were matched by other investment such a loss might therefore be unacceptable.

The table in Figure 5.2 provides a guide to a country's sustainable status but obviously needs to be treated with caution because sustainability requires more than simply replacing one type of resource with another.

Open Question

What resources should be on the critical list?

Open Question

What are the costs of using up critical resources?

Figure 5.2 The UK's sustainable development record 1980–1990 (% of GNP)

Year	S	$Detr.K_m$	$Dep. K_N + Deg. K_N$	Adjusted net savings sustainability index
1980	19.0	12.1	5.3	1.6
1981	18.1	12.4	6.2	−0.5
1982	17.6	12.0	6.3	−0.7
1983	17.8	11.8	6.6	−0.6
1984	17.6	11.8	7.2	−1.4
1985	18.4	11.7	6.5	0.2
1986	16.7	11.6	3.7	1.4
1987	16.7	11.3	3.8	1.6
1988	16.5	11.2	2.9	2.4
1989	16.5	10.9	2.8	3.7
1990	17.0	11.0	3.0	3.0

Source: David Pearce, R. Kerry Turner, Timothy O'Riordan, *Blueprint 3*, Earthscan, 1993

3 The impact of technology

Finding substitutes for non-renewable resources

Optical fibres: far beyond the limits

Optical fibres are made of a thin, flexible thread of glass, through which light can be beamed. A laser can vary the way that it produces light so that messages can be carried from one end of the fibre to the other. Complex pictures and images can be transmitted as well as text and speech. The optical fibre has opened the way to increasingly sophisticated communications systems which enable people to work in ways that have only recently been anticipated.

They have replaced the copper cable which has been used as the key means of communication since the introduction of telephones. Their advantages are significant:

■ They reduce our demand for copper, a non-renewable resource.

■ They take up far less space.

■ Their carrying capacity is vast: 16 fibres can carry all trans-Atlantic traffic; 50,000 messages can be carried at the same time.

■ They reduce the amount that people need to travel.

When industry finds that it is dependent on a raw material which may run out or become increasingly expensive, it starts the search for a replacement. The anticipated functioning of the market would lead to a price increase which makes this search necessary as the supply curve for a company's end product would be shifted to the left and the price would rise. A firm which finds an alternative would obviously be able to keep costs down and therefore have a competitive advantage.

Optical fibres have had a dramatic effect on the communications industry because achieving current usage levels would have involved the use of millions of tonnes of copper. World demand for copper may, in the long run, fall as a result, which means less damaging mining and slower use of a finite resource which can continue to be used when there is no substitute. Currently, however, the demand for copper is holding up because copper is still being used in the developing world. The capacity which optical fibre can provide is often beyond their needs. It also requires highly skilled technicians and considerable protection from the adverse conditions which will be encountered in some parts of the world.

There is, however, always a trade-off. By using less of a natural resource, there will be reduced demand for labour and capital equipment which is specifically designed for the industry. By imposing a carbon tax, the demand for coal would be reduced and therefore, mining communities would go into further decline. In future, copper miners might find themselves in the same position.

Using resources more effectively

The teleworker

A teleworker is an individual who works at home, part or full time, thanks to the benefit of modern technology. The optical fibre is again responsible for enabling this change to come about as the network can now cope, cheaply and effectively, with more lines. There are costs and benefits to the employee, the company and society as a whole from an increase in the number of teleworkers. In general it means that resources, both human and physical can be used more efficiently. Figure 5.3 shows the results of a major financial institution's pilot scheme, involving twenty senior managers and four secretaries.

Incorporated in the financial information are a variety of interesting gains to the company.

■ People worked harder and more efficiently at home.
■ People lost less time through illness.
■ People lost less time through travel delays.
■ Expensive training was not wasted as staff could continue on a part-time basis.
■ Office space could be used more efficiently.

The perceived drawback to the system was the fear of isolation among teleworkers. In the surveys which have been carried out this anxiety did not appear to be significant. There are some people who will never enjoy teleworking but it is a system which enables companies to push out their limits by using people and resources more effectively.

Figure 5.3 The financial case for teleworking

	Prior	Teleworking	Difference
	Costs per annum (£)		
Exceptional costs of change amortised over five years			
New equipment	None	71,000	71,000
Manager's time	None	2,450	2,450
Estimated loss of production time	None	44,800	44,800
External course/ consultants fees	None	1,000	1,000
Less retaining trained personnel		−50,000	−50,000

$$\frac{£69,250}{5} = -£13,850 \text{ per annum}$$

	Prior	Teleworking	Difference
Office space			
Rent	86,400		+86,400
Rates	21,600		+21,600
Electricity/air conditioning/heating	12,672	3,000	+9,672
Building maintenance	2,160		+2,160
Building insurance and security	10,080	4,000	+6,080
Wash rooms/ leisure facilities	2,496		+2,496
Time lost	13,440		+13,440
Clothing allowance	300		+300

	Prior	Teleworking	Difference
	Costs per annum (£)		
Commuting			
Running costs	18,894	3,750	+15,144
Train/bus fares adjustment +/– London Weighting	86,400	72,000	+14,400
Time lost/disruption	11,200		+11,200
Operating			
Secretarial salaries	56,000 (London)	28,000 (Local)	+28,000
Managers of teleworkers	131,600	171,080	−39,480
Gossip time	164,500		+164,500
Equipment and machines		As above	
Phones		As above	
Productivity up 11% on average			
Hours worked	1,410 hours	1,565 hours	155 hours
	987,000	1,095,500	108,500
Total savings per annum			444,412
Less exceptional costs			13,850
Total savings			**430,562**
Total saving per teleworker			**12,528**

Source: *The Economics of Teleworking*, British Telecom, 1993

The car is the means of transport for 85% of travel in the UK which represents a total of 556 billion kilometres each year – 40% of this is commuter travel. By facilitating the reduction of commuters, the gains would be considerable.

The benefits are not only concerned with allowing the company to function more efficiently but also assist the environment. In the mid-1990s approximately three million people were working at home and this reduces substantially, the number of commuters who drive to work. By encouraging people to work at home, society gains in the following ways:

■ 30 million gallons of fuel are burnt every day and as a result 2.4 billion gallons of exhaust gas are poured into the atmosphere. This contributes to the total amount of greenhouse gases from all sources. Increasing teleworkers by 15% would cut the amount of fuel burnt by 2.7 million gallons per workday which would be a direct gain not only to the atmosphere but also to our consumption of a non-renewable resource.

■ By removing a significant number of cars from the road each day, there would be less pressure to build new roads. As a result there would be less environmental deterioration.

■ The reduction in congestion would lead to a reduction in the time both goods and people spend on the roads and therefore reduce costs or prevent them rising.

■ Congestion increases the risk of accidents so fewer cars would cut the cost of hospital care, police time, insurance and the other subsidiary effects of collisions.

■ It may also have the effect of allowing people to work more effectively in rural areas and, therefore, reduce the pressures on housing and services in urban areas.

All these gains result from one key technological development – the optical fibre – which has opened new horizons for communications. It demonstrates well how the search for new ways of doing things can create benefits and extend the limits for individuals, companies and society as a whole.

4 The rise in productivity

Technological change usually involves an increase in productivity of people, raw material or capital goods. As a result, the amount that can be produced with a limited amount of resources is increased. There is, of course, an ultimate limit to the potential for increasing productivity. Something cannot be made from nothing but productivity is still rising

Investment

steadily throughout the world in many spheres. The most notable increases are in the East Asian countries, where rapid industrialisation has been taking place. Figure 5.4 shows this rise in productivity in the regions of the world.

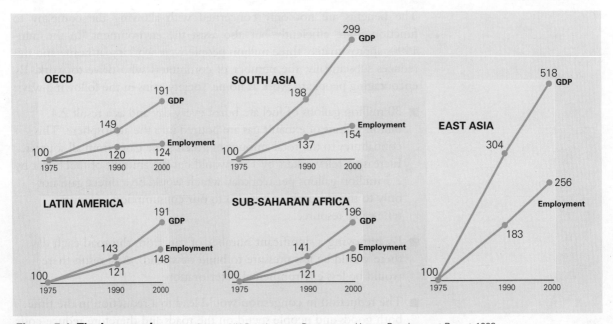

OECD
191 GDP
149
100 120 124 Employment
1975 1990 2000

SOUTH ASIA
299 GDP
198
154 Employment
100 137
1975 1990 2000

EAST ASIA
518 GDP
304
256 Employment
183
100
1975 1990 2000

LATIN AMERICA
191 GDP
143 Employment
148
100 121
1975 1990 2000

SUB-SAHARAN AFRICA
196 GDP
141 Employment
150
100 121
1975 1990 2000

Figure 5.4 The increase in productivity, 1975–2000

Source: UN Development Programme, *Human Development Report*, 1993

Computer control in production.

The greater productivity that is being achieved is, however, not without its costs. The countries of the Pacific Rim, which have shown such a dramatic rise have compromised their overall situation because of lack of care of the environment. They are beginning to realise the costs of the damage and changes are being made. If, however, growth is to become sustainable, economic and environmental policy will have to be looked at carefully.

Greater productivity depends partly on the quality of the work force. Highly sophisticated, computer controlled machinery often removes the need for unskilled people but needs to be operated by people with up to date, flexible skills. To achieve this flexibility, the workforce

Human capital

needs a high standard of education. The pattern which used to exist, of training for a job which you do for the rest of your life, is becoming a rare occurrence. Even in the same field, the work itself will change substantially in the course of a working life. Education and training must therefore allow people to cope with this changing scenario.

The one area in which it is difficult to achieve increases in productivity is the service sector. Technology has, however, been used effectively in the financial sector because it enables people to respond more quickly to market situations and permits transactions to be made more quickly. At the level of the local bank branch, transactions used to be recorded by hand as they were made at the till. At the close of business, it all had to be added up and checked carefully. Today, this process is done automatically as the customers pay money in or cash

Substitution

cheques. Cash machines reduce the need for labour because many transactions can now be carried out on a completely impersonal basis. It is, in fact, possible to carry out almost the entire banking function from a home computer terminal but this has not permeated the market yet.

Personal services are generally the ones which provide little scope for increasing productivity. A hairdresser cannot cut two people's hair at the same time so the limits are quite finite. There are a significant number of areas in which the need for the personal touch means that people will always have to be employed.

Open Question

Increasing productivity has helped to push out the limits but does it push out people as well?

Concern has been expressed about the trend to replace people with machines because it does not always lead to redeployment of the labour force. It has in recent years caused rising unemployment throughout the world. Pushing out the limits by creating a pool of people who are unlikely ever to find work may be an unwise strategy. The vista of a life of leisure as working hours fall has been on the horizon for many years but the reality at present is far less idyllic. As yet, society cannot cope effectively with a reduced requirement for people in industry.

5 The trend to services

As development progresses, the balance of economic activity tends to shift away from primary, towards the secondary and tertiary sectors. The poorest economies of the developing world are largely dependent on agriculture and as they grow, there is a shift to manufacturing industry. The countries of the developed world, however, have growing service sectors and steadily falling proportions of total resources concentrated in the primary and secondary sectors.

The countries in Figure 5.5 are described as 'high income economies' by the World Bank. They show this trend towards the service sector very clearly.

Figure 5.5 The shifting structure of production in high income economies

	Distribution of GDP %					
	Agriculture		Manufacturing		Services	
	1971	1991	1971	1991	1971	1991
Germany	3	2	38	23	47	59
Italy	8	3	27	21	51	64
Denmark	7	5	22	19	59	67
Finland	12	6	27	24	48	60
Japan	6	3	36	25	47	56
UK	3	2	33	21	53	70
Singapore	2	0	20	29	68	62

Source: World Bank, *World Development Report* 1993; *United Kingdom National Accounts*, HMSO, 1992

Singapore shows the trend in progress. It is a country which has recently joined the high income group and is still at the stage of having a growing manufacturing sector. The total size of the service sector has not fallen absolutely. The economy has been growing so rapidly that it has become a smaller proportion of the total, i.e. it has declined relatively.

In more affluent countries, demand for services increases. When people have all the modern conveniences, they turn to buying services. This means that they are buying people's time rather than resource intensive consumer goods. The quantity of resources that would be used if everyone in the developing world were to have a standard of living equivalent to those in the developed world is quite frightening. It is, however, worth remembering that the pattern of consumption changes as we become more affluent.

6 Alleviating poverty

Growth and equity

Despite continuous growth in much of the world, the number who are living in poverty is still increasing. Figure 5.6 shows the trend for the regions of the world to the year 2000. Only the Asian countries show a significant fall in those who are living below the poverty line. As the data for Eastern Europe do not include the people of the former USSR, it is difficult to judge the effect of the political changes which have taken place.

Figure 5.6 Poverty in the developing world

Region	% of population below the poverty line			Number of poor millions		
	1985	1990	2000	1985	1990	2000
South Asia	51.8	49.0	36.9	532	562	511
East Asia	13.2	11.3	4.2	182	169	73
Sub-Saharan Africa	47.6	47.8	49.7	184	216	304
Middle East and North Africa	30.6	33.1	30.6	60	73	89
Eastern Europe*	7.1	7.1	5.8	5	5	4
Latin America and the Caribbean	22.4	25.5	24.9	87	108	126

Note: *not including former USSR.
Source: World Bank, *World Development Report*, 1992

The data in Figure 5.6 show how inequitable the growth process has been. As most of the world has been growing richer, some regions such as Sub-Saharan Africa, the Middle East and North Africa, and Latin America and the Caribbean have become poorer. The projection to the year 2000 is based on the expected growth in GDP and assumes that the current pattern of income distribution will remain the same. A reversal of the trend is expected in the percentage of the population who are living below the poverty line in the last two but population growth, however, means that the total number of poor will still be increasing. In Sub-Saharan Africa both figures are expected to deteriorate.

This pattern of increasing disparity demonstrates the inequity which results from the existing trends in world development. The people who are falling below the poverty line are facing rising difficulties in finding enough to eat and maintain their families. Allied to this is the impact that their struggle has on the environment.

Poverty and the environment

Many of the world's poorest people live in regions that are environmentally vulnerable. In order to scratch a living, farmers have to use increasingly unsuitable land. This leads to erosion which exacerbates the problem for both the people and the environment. Poor people often do not have the resources to prevent the degradation of their land despite the fact that their culture may incorporate the ethics of stewardship of the traditional lands. As day to day survival is a struggle, worrying about tomorrow is a luxury that they cannot afford.

Urban poverty also leads to undesirable environmental effects. Inadequate sanitation and other services encourage disease and do not permit the residents to reap maximum benefit from assistance, such as education, which could improve their life style.

Industries in poor countries tend to have lower acceptable standards for pollution than in most of the developed world. Not only are local residents adversely affected but emissions from factories add disproportionately to the world total.

Figure 5.7 shows the relationship between income level and both urban sanitation and pollution. In both cases, the data shows an improving trend. On the pollution front, the rich countries are improving more quickly than the poor. As poor countries grow, sulphur dioxide emissions, for example, tend to rise. Eventually, after further growth, a point is reached when the government steps in and establishes limits so that improvements are made.

Figure 5.7 Environmental standards and income level

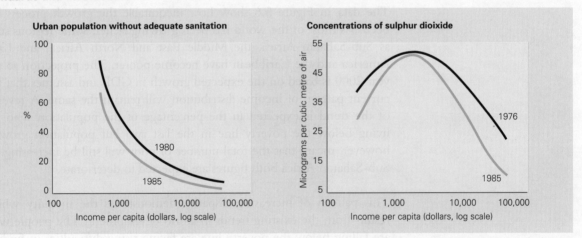

Source: World Bank, *World Development Report,* 1992

In the developed world, the pressure to look after the environment is increasing. In the developing world, the costs involved in such improvement mean that the trade off between shifting people from abject poverty and looking after the environment is still too great.

As the world develops, there are some challenges to be met if the pollution problem is not to get progressively worse. The targets that have been set allow developing countries some leeway because the standard of living must be dealt with first. In the Philippines, for example, manufacturing output is expected to grow nine or ten times by the year 2030 and the increase in the demand for electricity will be even more rapid. In order to maintain pollution at the current level, emissions will have to be cut by between 90% and 95%.

There are solutions to the problem as Figure 5.8 shows. The three lines on each graph each represent a different scenario. The top line shows the results of no change. The investment is highest in this category because it takes into account the social costs of extra pollution. The second line shows the effect of imposing efficiency reforms on existing techniques. Pollution rises more slowly and the level of investment required falls substantially. The bottom line shows the outcomes of using both efficiency reforms and abatement measures which involve the installation of clean technology. This has the most dramatic effect on the level of pollution and the cost is offset by the gains which result.

Figure 5.8 Scenarios for the expansion of electricity generation

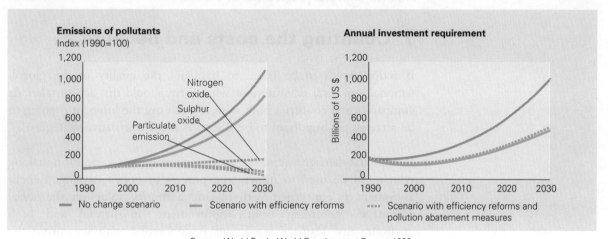

Source: World Bank, *World Development Report,* 1992

Delinking growth and pollution

Between 1970 and 1990, the economies of the OECD grew by 80%. Over this period, air quality has improved steadily:

- Particulate emissions   down 60%
- Sulphur oxides   down 38%
- Lead   down 50%

Many other persistent pollutants have been reduced and forested areas have increased. There are fewer large shipping accidents and oil spills. This has all occurred because of an annual increase in spending of between 0.8 and 1.5% on environmental protection. It has been divided approximately equally between the private and public sectors.

The process which has taken place is known as 'de-linking' growth from pollution. Despite the considerable improvement, the process is by no means complete. Water is still being polluted from agricultural chemicals, wet lands are still being destroyed and other natural habitats are suffering from encroachment. All this is endangering some animal and plant species and threatening others.

Although there is still much to be done, the process is under way and the experience will provide lessons for today's developing countries. The key factor is that it is often cheaper to prevent pollution than clean up the results.

If this de-linkage is to take place, alleviating poverty is crucial. Poverty leads to environmental degradation because people have no alternatives. By encouraging development which provides people with an improved standard of living, progress can be expected.

7 Counting the costs and benefits

If action needs to be taken to maintain the quality of the global, national and local environment what form should this action take? As companies and countries both wish to push out the limits, it is going to be increasingly important to be able to evaluate alternative strategies.

Benefit and damage assessment are one contribution to decision making which can be used to inform the process of policy making. Benefit assessment is concerned with placing a money value on the social advantages stemming from improvements in natural and built environments. Damage assessment is concerned with measuring the money losses to society resulting from deterioration of the environment. As environmental legislation increases, benefit and damage assessment will assist in upgrading the policy decisions.

Many of the gains from environmental policy do not show up in the form of immediate monetary gain: the benefits are to be found more in the quality of life than in any increment to a nation's economic output. But it is essentially an historical accident that some gains in human welfare are recorded in monetary terms in the national accounts and others are not. By and large, this is explained by the fact that the accounts measure gains to economic sectors in which property rights – whether private or public – have been well defined. The third party effects of economic activity – noise, air, water, pollution etc – do not show up in the accounts either because the ill-defined or absent rights to clean air, peace and quiet and pure water mean that no monetary transfer takes place between polluter and polluted, or because such transfers as do take place (e.g. through court action) are not part of the national accounting conventions. Thus environmental benefits tend to be less 'concrete', more 'soft' than market place benefits. The temptation is to downgrade them by comparison. – Source: David Pearce and Anil Markandya, *Environmental Policy Benefits: Monetary Valuation*, OECD,1989

There are a range of strategies which can be used in this process.

Cost–benefit analysis (CBA) looks at the monetary value of benefits in order to compare them with the monetary value of costs (which should reflect the value to society of the resources being used up) in any project or activity. The requirement for a policy to be worth proceeding with is that benefits are greater than costs. Cost–benefit analysis therefore supports the drive towards economic efficiency. Cost–benefit analysis tries to weight the costs and benefits which are implicit in people's economic choices.

The basic rule of CBA is that a policy or activity is desirable if benefits exceed costs. However, there are many criticisms of CBA which revolve around the difficulty of putting money values on things that are difficult to quantify.

Cost-effectiveness analysis involves measuring costs in money terms but not benefits. Such a technique can be used to decide which might be the most appropriate choice from a number of options but it cannot measure whether the benefits to society outweigh the costs.

If, for example, there is £1 million available for saving lives by improved health screening the method of carrying out the screening which will be chosen, is the one which uses the money most effectively.

Multi-criteria analysis can be used when there are a number of outputs which stem from a particular policy or activity which are measured using different units. It therefore becomes necessary to attach a 'weighting' to the importance of each of the outputs. For example, if reduced accidents are more important than gains in scenic beauty then they will be given a higher weighting. The weights then play the part of prices reflecting the relative importance of each of the outputs considered.

Risk–benefit analysis is simply cost–benefit analysis transferred to risky events e.g. nuclear accidents, health risks from chemicals on the soil etc. For example, if the government or a business organisation takes no action to reduce the amount of chemicals in drinking water the risks or costs might be the cancers that result. The benefits of 'no-action' are the avoided resource costs of removing the chemicals.

Decision analysis can be used to work through the impact of various decisions. Values can be attached to the potential results of the alternative strategies in order to quantify the impact of changes or policies. A decision tree with various branches can be followed through to assess the expected values of particular choices. Clearly the values ascribed to different alternatives may depend on subjective estimations of possible effects.

Environmental-impact assessment involves identifying and measuring the impacts of actions which are either harmful or beneficial. It is particularly concerned with environmental decision making. EIA may or may not involve ascribing monetary values to the environmental impacts of activities or policies.

Weighing up the 'total economic value' of the environment

In the 1990s the value of the environment has increasingly come to be recognised.

David Pearce has argued that the Total Economic Value of a resource should be measured by:

Total Economic Value = Total User Benefits + Total Intrinsic Benefits

User benefits are made up of *consumptive* and *non-consumptive values*. For example, a hunter might benefit from consuming the products of hunting in a wildlife park. Someone else might prefer simply to enjoy the view and the magnificent scenery, in other words, to benefit from non-consumptive values.

Other people benefit from environmental assets through *indirect use* e.g. by reading about the wildlife park, or seeing a film about it. These values are positive and may be regarded as intrinsic values of the wildlife asset. Other people still benefit from the existence of environmental assets such as wildlife parks even though they will never experience or enjoy them themselves. They feel good if these wonderful resources are preserved for other people and for future generations.

This altruistic benefit also can be seen as a bequest to non-human populations such as animals – people receive benefits from 'Saving the whale', 'Saving the white rhino', etc.

David Pearce and others have identified a number of sophisticated techniques for measuring the value of environmental benefits. Direct valuation techniques involve measuring the money value of environmental gains, e.g. better air quality, improved scenic views, etc.

Hedonic valuation involves calculating how much people are prepared to pay for an improvement in environmental quality (and the social value of such an improvement).

Contingent valuation involves asking people what they are willing to pay for a benefit, and/or what they are willing to receive by way of compensation to tolerate a cost.

Indirect valuation techniques are used when it is not possible to place a direct value on an environmental good usually because it is impossible to make such a linkage because, for example, many people are unaware of the effect of air pollution on their health. Indirect valuation involves calculating a *dose-response* relationship between pollution and some effect. Dose-response involves estimating damage actually done perhaps through measuring the numbers of deaths due to sulphur dioxide pollution.

8 Achieving the unachievable?

Trade-offs

Countries, companies and individuals are all striving to push out the limits. Much of the activity is benign as they look for greater efficiency and increased productivity. However, if left to its own devices, the market will often sacrifice the external factors in order to enhance private benefit. When this happens, the government needs to step in to restore the balance. The strategies which have been discussed in earlier Enquiries need to be put to work.

The decision-making process is not, however, straight forward. Environmental degradation is not easily quantifiable and the causal relationships are not always clear. The cause of many problems is cumulative. The build up of pollutants, for example, or the range of factors which contribute to a problem mean that it is often difficult to identify a single cause. If suspicions are proved in the future it may be too late to correct the damage that has been done so precautions must be taken now.

Open Question

Should fair-skinned people of the developed world be asked to stay out of the sun to avoid skin cancer so that cheap refrigeration can remain available to the poor of the developing world?

Sustainable growth is only possible if potential problems are taken into account but trade offs may have to be made in order to avoid increasing inequalities. CFCs, for example, are suspected of destroying the ozone layer. There are still aspects of the relationship that scientists do not understand but it is currently accepted that the risks involved in ignoring the problem are too great. By banning CFCs, refrigeration will become more expensive because of the costs of alternative coolants. The effect on the developing world may therefore be deleterious as food poisoning may increase because of the problems of keeping food in hot countries.

Trade-offs will also be required when it comes to making decisions about the best strategy for using available resources. No country has unlimited resources and their allocation has to be worked out carefully if the optimum outcome is to be achieved. The trade-off discussed above is a difficult one to evaluate because of the uncertainty but on smaller issues evaluation of costs and benefits can provide helpful information to assist in decision making. The case study of a decision in Poland demonstrates this.

Sulphur dioxide or particulates?

In Tarnobrzeg in Poland, the costs and benefits of pollution control were compared in order to decide the priorities. The economic benefits to the local population in terms of mortality and morbidity as well as material damage and soiling were compared with the cost of preventive measures. Figure 5.9 shows the outcomes.

It was discovered that the costs of reducing sulphur dioxide were, at all levels, greater than the benefits, whereas the benefits of reducing particulate matter were, at all levels, greater than the costs. Therefore, at a local level, it was wise to invest in the reduction of particulate matter.

Figure 5.9 Costs and benefits of pollution control in Tarnobrzeg

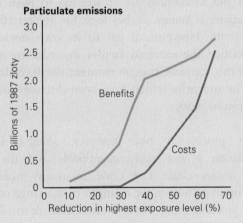
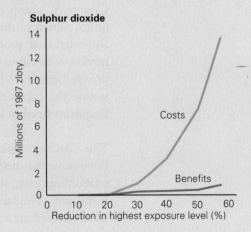

Source: World Bank, *World Development Report*, 1992

Corporate responsibility

A key factor in achieving what might have been regarded as unachievable is the growing realisation by business that responsibility for the environment can be beneficial to the efficiency of both production and sales. In the US, the growth of environmental management has become part of the move to total quality. Many companies have already discovered that it is cheaper to correct faults before goods leave the factory and many are discovering that it is better still to make products without faults. The customer who receives a 'Friday' car is not a good ambassador for any company and the cost involved in sorting out the problems is always high. The same logic works with environmental issues. By building sound environmental practice into the production system, costs can be cut in the long run. It is almost always more expensive to add filters after the factory has been opened than to incorporate them from the start. Better still, by looking carefully at the inputs, it may be possible to minimise pollutant outputs.

Many companies are setting standards for world wide subsidiaries so that the standards which are demanded in the developed world are increasingly being sought in the developing world. As waste is always expensive to deal with, monitoring the output and accounting for the cost often encourages firms to take a more positive approach to adjusting the methods of production.

The production process has become inseparable from the marketing side because as consumers' awareness rises, they want to know about the environmental aspects relating to the making of the product. By meeting stringent standards, the company, therefore, has a positive sales advantage.

There is pressure from most stakeholders to improve standards in this way. The retail market is the one which has generally been thought of as the green driving force but increasingly industrial companies are putting pressure on their suppliers to meet more stringent standards. ICI, for example, takes contaminated sulphuric acid back from its customers in the oil industry in order to clean it up. A company which deals in this way will attract customers because it assists in the solution of environmental problems.

Many companies are starting to build the achievement of environmental standards into their rewards packages. The failure to meet such standards may lead to the loss of bonuses. This signals to the staff, the degree of importance that the company gives to the issue.

By looking carefully at the environmental aspects of the production process and searching for ways in which it might be improved, a company is enabling growth to continue. If industry in general does not take care of the environment, all the strategies for growth which might be developed will become futile because countries will have to struggle to maintain the current standard of living. If the market fails to provide an adequate incentive for companies to carry out this work, governments and international organisations have to step in to encourage them with strategies which have been discussed in earlier Enquiries.

The environmentalist's dream and the capitalist's drive

Let me deliberately polarise the argument (about pathways to growth) and call them the 'environmentalist's dream' and the 'capitalist's drive'.

The 'environmentalist's dream' looks for radical change in economic patterns and lifestyles so as to dramatically reduce consumption in the industrialised world and free resources for developing nations. For those alienated by the complexities of modern industrial and mass-consumer society, it is a beguiling prospect. But is it politically or practically possible? Can we turn back the clock to some pre-industrial Arcady and forgo the living standards that late 20th century industrialised society has come to take for granted, and millions less fortunate to aspire to? There is no sign that voters anywhere are prepared to accept this – rather we measure our politicians by their capacity to deliver economic growth and prosperity. Nor is it clear that the emerging economies of the developing world would benefit from our economic stagnation. I think the reverse is more probably true.

We need to have a clear idea of the mechanisms to deliver investment in long-term environmental improvement – to clean up the legacy of the past, to develop new, cleaner plants and processes for the future, and to spread this technology around the globe.

The mechanism that can deliver such change is what I called the 'capitalist drive' – of businesses competing freely within the wealth creation process. This is what has driven the continual technological innovation that has transformed the material standards of expanding populations over the past three centuries. It is, I believe, the only dynamic that can deliver the investment and technological advances necessary.

Of course, governments have a right and a duty to regulate for environmental and other societal goals. But I would stress the necessity – which I think few outside business really comprehend – of working within the disciplines of the market. If, in the rush to do something – anything – to protect the environment, we do things which damage the ability of companies to compete, to be profitable, to fund new investment, to pay a return to those who provide capital, then we will stifle their capacity for environmental advance.

Source: Part of a speech made by Sir John Collins, Chair and Chief Executive of Shell UK Limited, to the Institute of Energy Conference, July 1993

Getting it right

Achieving sustainability is concerned with achieving a balance between the use of resources and their replacement. The scale of the economy is only one of the issues involved in the process. The others which are shown in Figure 5.10 are represented by the boxes in the middle line of the diagram.

The structure of the economy is concerned with the type of goods and services which are produced. This will change as economies become increasingly mature and the focus shifts from agriculture to manufacturing and then to services.

The input–output efficiency shows how effectively an economy uses its factors of production. By improving this, a company or country can affect resource utilisation and therefore the degree of sustainability. An alternative strategy would be to develop new techniques which mean substitutes can be used for increasingly scarce resources.

Technology also has a role in producing new methods of reducing environmental damage.

Figure 5.10
The inter-relationships

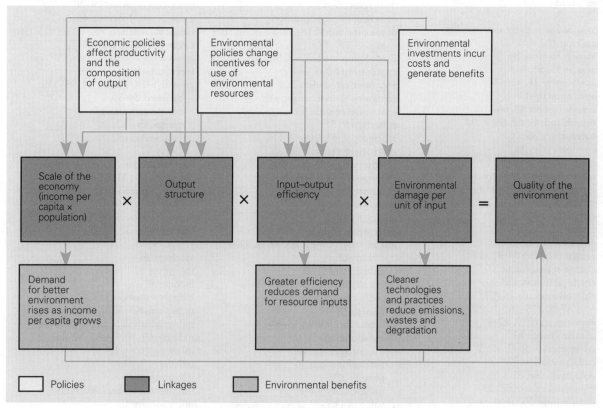

Source: World Bank, *World Development Report*, 1992

The boxes at the top of the diagram show how government policy can be used to help create the balance when the market fails and those at the bottom show the benefits that can be reaped. All these factors together contribute to improving the quality of the environment. The limits to growth are therefore not insuperable provided that the relationships between individuals, companies and the government result in resources being used efficiently. The prospects for future growth overcoming the limits depend on the successful combination of markets and government. The market will encourage firms to be creative and devise strategies to cope with resource limitation while governments need to use their influence to ensure that critical areas are not at the mercy of the excesses of the market.

Index